18/04/19

Please return / renew this item
by the last date shown.
Books may also be renewed by
phone or the Internet.

Tel: 0161 254 7777

www.manchester.gov.uk/libraries

Top 10 Algarve Highlights

The Top 10 of Everything

CONTENTS

The Algarve Area by Area

Streetsmart

Within each Top 10 list in this book, no hierarchy of quality or popularity is implied. All 10 are, in the editor's opinion, of roughly equal merit.

Title page, front cover and spine Rocky outcrops along Ponta da Piedade, Lagos
Back cover, clockwise from top left Grilled sardines; Sunset at Rio Gilão; A woman traveller in Faro; Towering outcrops; Sandy beach near Lagos

Welcome to
The Algarve

With its golden beaches, fabulous golf courses and year-round appeal, the Algarve is an enticing holiday destination. This enchanting region is famous for its stunning ochre-splashed coastline of shallow bays, vertiginous cliffs and lively resorts, and is also home to a verdant canvas of rolling countryside, quiet villages and sleepy hamlets. With Eyewitness Top 10 Algarve, it's yours to explore.

Busiest during the summer, the warm, crystalline waters of the Algarve lure beachgoers to its southern shores. You can hike or cycle nature trails through the serene **Parque Natural da Ria Formosa**, take in majestic views from the top of **Monchique**, or kayak in the grottoes off **Lagos**. Besides the beautiful landscape, the region has many cultural attractions, including the **Palácio da Galeria** in **Tavira**, the mighty Moorish castle of **Silves** and the gilded medieval interior of **Sé Cathedral** in **Faro**.

Travelling the Algarve's hinterland is to journey through a landscape embroidered with cork-oak and citrus trees. Eucalyptus scents the air. Visitors can enjoy tastings at some excellent wineries. An unhurried way of life prevails and many of the region's traditional festivals and ceremonies take place on this strip of coast. Colourful market towns such as **Loulé** enhance the local flavour.

Whether you're visiting for a weekend or a week, our Top 10 guide brings together the best of everything the Algarve has to offer. The guide has useful tips throughout, from seeking out what's free to avoiding the crowds, plus six easy-to-follow itineraries, designed to tie together a clutch of sights in a short space of time. An additional chapter on the **Alentejo** highlights the region's neighbouring province. Add inspiring photography and detailed maps, and you've got the essential pocket-sized travel companion. **Enjoy the book, and enjoy the Algarve**.

Clockwise from top: **Praia da Dona Ana, Lagos; Sé Cathedral, Faro; a cobbled street in Alte; boats at Praia dos Pescadores, Albufeira; octopus pots, Santa Luzia; the town of Monchique; Praia dos Pescadores, Albufeira**

Exploring the Algarve

A favourite year-round holiday destination, the Algarve has much to offer visitors. Celebrated for its fantastic beaches and lively resorts, the Algarve has an equally enticing interior just waiting to be discovered. Here are a few ideas for a two-day and a week-long stay, which will help you to make the most of coast and country.

Faro Old Town's pretty cobbled streets make for an enjoyable stroll.

Aljezur
Fóia · Monchique
Parque Natural do Sudoeste Alentejano e Costa Vicentina
Caldas de Monchique
Silves
Portimão
Meia Praia
Lagos
Praia da Rocha
Albufeira
Pre
da Ou
Cabo de São Vicente
Praia do Martinhal
Sagres

Key
— Two-day itinerary
— Seven-day itinerary

Two Days in the Algarve

Day ❶
MORNING
Start in **Faro** with some sightseeing in the Old Town (see pp12–13). Ponder ancient artifacts at the Museu Municipal de Faro and follow with a visit to the handsome 13th-century Sé. Afterwards, climb the cathedral's bell tower and enjoy the views across the wetlands.
AFTERNOON
Have lunch at Faz Gostos (Rua do Castelo 13; 289 878 422), and then join a boat cruise (see pp58–9) through the protected **Parque Natural da Ria Formosa** (see pp30–33). End the day exploring **Faro's New Town** (see pp14–15) and strolling by the riverfront.

Day ❷
MORNING
Travel east to **Tavira** (see pp16–17) and begin by perusing the Núcleo

Islâmico. Climb the hill to the Moorish castle (see p45) for splendid rooftop views. Next, look for the tombs of Crusader knights in Igreja de Santa Maria do Castelo. Meander back to the river, the Rio Gilão, and take in views of the photogenic Ponte Romana.
AFTERNOON
Stop for lunch at **Brisa do Rio** (see p95) then recharge on **Ilha de Tavira** (see p94), reached by ferry from Quatro Águas quay.

Seven Days in the Algarve

Day ❶ and ❷
Follow the two-day Algarve itinerary.

Day ❸
Travel early to **Loulé** (see pp22–3) and browse the market if it is a Saturday. Visit the bewitching Ermida de Nossa Senhora da Conceição

A vast swathe of golden sand is set against dramatic multicoloured cliffs at Praia da Rocha in Portimão.

The spa hamlet of Caldas de Monchique has been famous for the restorative powers of its water since Roman times.

before continuing west to **Albufeira** (see pp36–7). Take some time to relax on Praia da Oura, and then dance the night away at **Libertos** (see p67) on the neon-lit "Strip".

Day ❹

Continue to **Lagos** (see pp26–7), where it is easy to spend a few hours in the fascinating Museu Municipal Dr José Formosinho. Take a cruise to the sea caves at Ponta da Piedade. Back on land, head for the sand on **Meia Praia** (see p49), then enjoy an evening drink at a bar on the **Frente Ribeirinha** (see p27).

Day ❺

Drive further west to **Sagres** (see pp34–5). Delve into history at the mysterious Fortaleza de Sagres. Afterwards, follow the bracing Ponta de Sagres Panoramic Walk. Linger in the afternoon on sheltered **Praia do Martinhal** (see p102). For a dramatic

finale, drive over to windblown **Cabo de São Vicente** (see p35) for awe-inspiring ocean vistas.

Day ❻

Journey north through the **Parque Natural do Sudoeste Alentejano e Costa Vicentina** (see p100). Turn inland at **Aljezur** (see p101) for the quaint spa hamlet of **Caldas de Monchique** (see p99). Continue to **Monchique** (see pp20–21). Saunter through its steep, narrow streets to shop for cadeiras de tesoura (see p104). End the day with great views from the peak of **Fóia** (see p20).

Day ❼

Arrive in **Silves** (see pp18–19). Allow time to absorb the excellent Museu Municipal de Arqueologia. For a more tangible sense of history, amble up to the impressive castle (see p44). Use the afternoon to visit **Portimão** (see pp38–9), before relaxing on Praia da Rocha.

Top 10 Algarve Highlights

The quayside at the village of Ferragudo

🔟 Algarve Highlights

The Moors called their al-Gharb the Sunset Land. Blessed with a mild winter climate and lots of sunny days, Portugal's playground province remains one of the most popular year-round holiday destinations in Southern Europe. Lively coastal resorts spill over ribbons of golden sand, whilst quiet, traditional villages can be found inland.

Faro **1**
Faro is the capital of the Algarve and an important tourist and commercial centre. Its historic quarter overlooks a marina and the Ria Formosa *(see pp12–15)*.

Tavira **2**
Nearly 40 churches can be found in this elegant riverside town, which is one of the prettiest and most romantic places to be found in the Algarve. The Gilão River, spanned by a Roman bridge, flows through the centre *(see pp16–17)*.

Silves **3**
Once the grandiose capital of the Moorish province of al-Gharb, Silves today is dominated by the ochre ramparts of its huge castle. Lush orange groves blanket the country-side *(see pp18–19)*.

Monchique **4**
The Serra de Monchique rises 458 m (1,500 ft), enveloping the hillside town of Monchique and its neighbouring spa centre *(see pp20–21)*.

5 Loulé

A gateway to the central hinterland and the Caldeirão mountain range, Loulé hosts a daily market and is a thriving centre for the sale of local handicrafts (see pp22–3).

6 Lagos

A young, vibrant and carefree spirit imbues this resort. The nearby beaches, punctuated with outcrops of sandstone rock, are spectacular (see pp26–9).

0 km 15
0 miles 15

Martim Longo · 124
Alcoutim
Vaqueiros ·
IC27
122
Rio Guadiana
Ameixial ·
Cachopo
Odeleite
Serra de Alcaria do Cume
Salir
Barranco do Velho
Azinhal
São Brás de Alportel
Castro Marim
Vila Real de S. António
Loulé 5 · 270
A22
Conceição
125
Almancil · Estói · Moncarapacho
2 Tavira
Vilamoura
Olhão
Fuseta
Quinta do Lago
✈ 1 Faro
7 Parque Natural da Ria Formosa

7 Parque Natural da Ria Formosa

A sanctuary for a wealth of bird and animal life, this is one of the most important wetland zones in Europe (see pp30–33).

8 Sagres

This town sits on an isolated promontory pounded by the Atlantic. Dramatic views of the ocean from the Cabo de São Vicente (see pp34–5).

9 Albufeira

This is the Algarve's largest resort. Generous beaches flank bustling esplanades brimming with cafés and trendy clubs (see pp36–7).

10 Portimão

Dating back to pre-Roman times, Portimão has an attractive 18th-century town centre and a broad esplanade, which overlooks the River Arade (see pp38–9).

TOP 10 ⭐ Faro Old Town

Faro's venerable Cidade Velha (Old Town) is the city's most interesting quarter and can be appreciated at a leisurely pace on foot. Set within a circle of medieval walls, the whole vicinity is a veritable time capsule reflecting Faro's brief golden age in the 16th century. The landmark cathedral and cloistered convent are set alongside a patchwork of narrow, cobbled streets with several inviting cafés and shops.

6 Sé (Cathedral)
The interior of the 13th-century cathedral **(below)** reveals a spectacular fusion of the Gothic, Renaissance and Baroque styles: the Capela de Nossa Senhora dos Prazeres, especially, is a jewel of Baroque art, with gilded and lacquered wood carvings, inlaid marble and polished *azulejos*.

1 Museu Municipal de Faro
Gargoyles in the shape of animals embellish the delightfully secluded Renaissance cloisters of this former convent *(see p46)* **(above)**, now home to the town's archaeological museum. Highlights include a huge Roman floor mosaic and a collection of Moorish oil lamps.

3 Igreja de São Francisco
Stunning panels of *azulejos* (painted tiles) depicting the life of St Francis adorn the walls of this church. The vault contains a polychrome panel showing the coronation of the Virgin.

4 Arco da Vila
This grandiose archway to the Old Town was inaugurated in 1812. Tucked inside the arch is an 11th-century horseshoe gate, which is believed to have been built by the Moors and is the only one of its kind in the Algarve.

2 Paço Episcopal
The original building was plundered and damaged by the Earl of Essex in 1596. Rebuilt again after the 1755 earthquake, it is still in use today, but closed to the public **(above)**.

5 Centro Interpretativo do Arco da Vila
The museum housed within the arch **(right)** chronicles the history of Faro and is set across two floors. The rooftop terrace affords grand views of the monument and the Old Town.

9 Galeria Trem

Part of a former military barracks, the Trem art gallery shares floor space with an excavated Roman arch built on Moorish foundations. The venue is a favourite among modern artists.

7 Igreja da Misericórdia

Built on the site of a 16th-century chapel, the church **(above)** houses a small museum. The highlight is the 17th-century altar, which features a splendid triumphal arch decorated in gilded rococo carvings. Adjoining the church is an 18th-century hospital, but is closed to the public.

Old Town

8 Walls and Towers

The original castle walls are vestiges of the Roman occupation of the town, but the rest of the fortifications are the result of 16th-century labour. The exception is the Byzantine towers, added after the collapse of the Roman Empire.

10 Ermida de Nossa Senhora do Ó

The medieval "Chapel of the Pregnant Virgin", is hidden away in the Arco da Vila. It hosts live performances featuring the Portuguese guitar, which is the instrument behind the unique sound of fado.

THE STORY OF FARO

The Phoenicians and Carthaginians established trading posts on the banks of the Ria Formosa, which grew into a major Roman port known as Ossonoba. The Moors fortified the town but couldn't halt the armies of Afonso III, who captured the city in 1249. A period of prosperity ended in 1596 when the Earl of Essex burned the city. Rebuilding began, but the 1755 earthquake destroyed it again, forever altering the urban make-up.

NEED TO KNOW
MAP K6

Tourist information:
by harbour; (289) 803 604; 9:30am–5:30pm Mon–Fri, 9:30am–1pm & 2–6pm Sat & Sun

Museu Municipal de Faro: Largo Dom Afonso III; 10am–7pm Tue–Fri (6pm winter), 11:30am–6pm Sat & Sun (winter: 10:30am–5pm); adm

Igreja de São Francisco: 10am–noon Mon–Fri

Igreja da Misericórdia: Praça Dom Francisco Gomes 17; 9am–1pm Mon–Fri

Ermida de Nossa Senhora do Ó: noon, 3pm & 4:30pm Sun–Thu; adm (under-12s free)

■ The 16th-century Porta Nova is near the embarkation point for boat cruises on the Ria Formosa *(see p59).*

■ Cathedral entry includes access to the bell tower.

■ Entry to the Arco da Vila centre is via the tourist office, with both sharing the same hours.

Faro New Town and Riverfront

Baroque façade of Igreja do Carmo

1 Igreja do Carmo/ Capela dos Ossos

MAP U1 ■ Largo do Carmo ■ Closed Sun ■ Adm

A feast of Baroque decoration, gilded with the finest Brazilian gold leaf. A macabre offering, though, is the church's Capela dos Ossos (Chapel of Bones), which is lined with the skulls and bones of more than a thousand monks.

2 Teatro Lethes

MAP U2 ■ Rua de Portugal 58 ■ (289) 878 908 ■ www.teatro lethes.com

Once a Jesuit college, this little Italianate gem dates from 1874 and is a beautiful example of a late 19th-century provincial play-house. It hosts plays and concerts. Guided tours can be arranged.

3 Parque Ribeirinho

MAP K6

Located behind the railway station, Parque Ribeirinho overlooks the Ria Formosa. The park is excellent for walking and cycling.

4 Science Alive Centre

MAP T3 ■ Rua Comandante Francisco Manuel ■ Closed Mon ■ Adm ■ www.ccvalg.pt

An engrossing interactive study centre, which promotes scientific and technological awareness. Climb up to the centre's "observatory" for a voyage into the Milky Way.

5 Faro Jewish Heritage Centre

MAP K5 ■ Estrada da Penha ■ Open 9am–1pm & 2–5pm Mon–Fri ■ www.cilisboa.org/hist_faro

The city's 19th-century Jewish cemetery is laid out in the traditional Sephardic way. The informative Isaac Bitton Synagogue Museum is adjacent to the cemetery, and is decorated with original furniture from 1820.

6 Museu Regional do Algarve

MAP U2 ■ Praça da Liberdade ■ Open 10am–1:30pm & 2:30–5:30pm Mon–Fri ■ Adm

Find out about life in rural Algarve through this display of traditional arti-facts. Paintings by Faro artist Carlos Porfírio are also on display here.

Display, Museu Regional do Algarve

7 Ermida de Santo António do Alto

MAP W1 ■ Rua da Berlim

Built in 1355, this is one of the oldest buildings in Faro. A climb up the steps at the side of the chapel rewards visitors with a rooftop view.

8 Ilha de Faro
MAP K6

A natural link in a chain of sand-dune islands that constitute part of the Parque Natural da Ria Formosa (see pp30–33). The estuary side of the beach, with its sheltered waters, is popular with watersports enthusiasts.

Mosaics at Villa Romana de Milreu

9 Palácio Bívar
MAP T2 ◼ Rua Conselheiro Bívar

This late 18th-century former private residence, with attractive balconied windows and a grand portal, is generally regarded as the finest example of Neo-Classical architecture in the Algarve.

10 Villa Romana de Milreu
MAP K5

Just 5 km (3 miles) north of Faro, the Roman remains at Milreu (see p93) include the ruins of a luxury villa and baths dating from the 2nd century AD.

COSMOPOLITAN FARO

Faro's history (see p13) and cosmopolitan flavour continues beyond the obvious Moorish and Christian features of the old town. New townhouses sprang up outside the city walls in the 17th and 18th centuries, Mannerist in style. Battlements built during the War of Restoration (1640–68) enclosed this new urban area. Present day Faro cap-italizes on a vibrant social life and a rich artistic heritage. Alluring historical buildings can be found alongside modern museums and quaint pavement cafés. The city boasts a colourful agenda of music and dance; as exciting, in fact, as the city's restaurants, that serve the best traditional cuisine of the Algarve.

Afonso III, King of Portugal

FARO'S TOP 10 PERSONALITIES

1 Mohammed ben Said ben Hárun gave Faro its name in the 11th century.

2 Afonso III captured the city in 1249.

3 Samuel Gacon produced the first printed manuscript in Portugal (1487).

4 Queen Catarina completed Convento de Nossa Senhora da Assunção.

5 The 2nd Earl of Essex sacked Faro in 1596.

6 Bishop Francisco Gomes (1739–1816) rebuilt the city after the quake.

7 Francisco Xavier Fabri (1761–1817) was a famous Neo-Classical architect.

8 Manuel Bívar (1861–1901) was a key member of an illustrious family.

9 Dr Amadeu Ferreira de Almeida Carvalho (1876–1966) gave his art collection to the public.

10 Carlos Porfírio (1895–1970) was a renowned modern artist.

Faro's attractive marina is the starting point for popular boat cruises on the lagoon.

🔟 ⭐ Tavira

With its timeless atmosphere, traditional character and dignified charm, it is small wonder that many consider the elegant riverside town of Tavira to be the most pleasant and picturesque in the Algarve. Sited on both sides of the Rio Gilão, the town is perhaps best known for its abundance of churches – nearly 40 in all. Tavira's prosperity today relies to a great degree on tourism, although not to the detriment of the town's peaceful ambience.

1 Castle Remains
The surviving walls of this Moorish fort envelop a spruce garden. The view from the ramparts takes in the town's *(see p45)* pyramid-shaped rooftops and distant Ilha de Tavira.

Tavira

LARGO DO TREM
RUA J. PESSOA
PRAÇA DA REPÚBLICA Rio Gilão
R. DO CAIS
R. JOSÉ PIRES PADINHA
R. DA LIBERDADE
3 km (2 miles) ➤ **7**

4 Igreja de Santa Maria do Castelo
The clock face of this church is a familiar landmark **(left)**. Inside are the tombs of the Moors' nemesis, Dom Paio Peres Correia, and seven of his knights.

2 Casa Fotografia Andrade
This permanent exhibition, consisting of photographs taken by the Andrade family, chronicles life in Tavira from the 20th century onwards.

5 Torre de Tavira – Camera Obscura
Housed at the top of an old water tower, the camera obscura focuses a live 360-degree image of the city onto a huge screen.

6 Ponte Romana
The foundations of the low, arched stone bridge **(above)** spanning the Rio Gilão are Roman in origin. Illuminated at night, creating a romantic ethereal glow, the bridge is a favourite subject for artists.

3 Igreja da Misericórdia
Townsfolk are justifiably proud that this 16th-century church **(below)** is considered to be the Algarve's most important Renaissance monument.

7 Ilha de Tavira
A regular ferry service offers an easy escape to the marvellous sand-dune island, which is popular during the summer months for its excellent swimming. It lies within the Parque Natural da Ria Formosa *(see pp30–33)*.

8 Núcleo Islâmico

Tavira's Islamic heritage is featured at this museum. A video presentation outlines the history behind the artifacts, which date from the time when Tavira was ruled by the Moors. The 11th-century Tavira Vase **(right)** is a highlight.

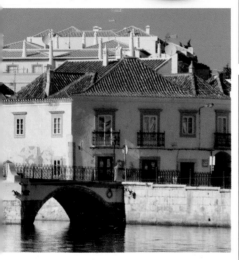

9 Palácio da Galeria

Works by Picasso and Paula Rego have been exhibited at this contemporary gallery, housed in a refurbished 16th-century palace. The palace is set on Moorish foundations, vestiges of which are displayed under a glass floor in the entrance hall.

10 Convento da Graça

Now a luxury *pousada (see p123)*, this 16th-century building *(see p126)* **(below)** is characterized by a rich mix of Renaissance and Baroque architecture, with the cloister. The remains of a 12th-century Moorish street can also be seen from the bar.

LOCAL CUISINE

Tavira's seafood specialities include *açorda marisco*, a concoction of cockles, prawns and clams sunk in a thick bread-based soup, and *lulas recheadas*, which is tender squid filled with cured meats and rice, braised in an onion and tomato sauce. Santa Luzia, a village southwest of Tavira, is said to be the Algarve's octopus capital. Order the octopus rice stew *(arroz de polvo)*.

NEED TO KNOW
MAP M4

Tourist information: Praça da República 5; (281) 322 511; open 9:30am–1pm & 2–5:30pm daily (winter hours vary)

Casa Fotografia Andrade: Rua da Liberdade 36; (281) 322 102; open 10am–1pm & 3–7pm Mon–Fri, 10am–1pm Sat; adm

Igreja da Misericórdia: open 9am–noon & 2–5pm Mon, 9am–12:30pm & 2–5:30pm Tue–Sun; closed Oct–May Sun; adm

Torre de Tavira – Camera Obscura: www.torredetavira.com

Núcleo Islâmico: Praça da República; (281) 320 568; open 9:15am–4:30pm Tue–Sat; adm

Palácio da Galeria: Calçada da Galeria; (281) 320 540; open 9am–4:30pm Tue–Sat; adm

• Vila Galé Albacora's Udiving Centre *(see p125)* welcomes divers of all abilities (www.udiving.pt).

• Grab drinks and snacks at Café Veneza, on Praça da República.

⭐ Silves

Known as Xelb in Arabic, the 30,000-strong Moorish settlement prospered until 1189, when Dom Sancho I laid siege to it with the help of an English crusader army. The Christians finally gained total control in 1242. These days, Silves is better known as a centre of citrus fruit and cork production. The castle, with its sandstone walls casting a sepia wash over the town below, is a stark reminder of Silves' once-powerful past.

Castelo ①

The grandest monument (see p44) to Islamic rule in the Algarve, Silves Castle **(right)** is a huge strong-hold built on the site of 4th-century Roman fortifications. Views from the ramparts are superb.

Sé (Cathedral) ②

Dating from the 13th century, the town's Gothic cathedral **(above)** was the seat of the Algarve see until 1577, when that honour was transferred to the bishops' palace in Faro. Curiosities include gargoyles on the apse and Crusader tombs.

Museu Municipal de Arqueologia ③

This fascinating museum (see p46) superbly charts human existence in the region from the Palaeolithic period to the 16th century.

④ Ancient Pillory

A common symbol of municipal power across all of Portugal, the pillory standing near the castle was rebuilt from 16th-century remains. Topped by a decorative crown with four sinewy, wrought-iron dragons jutting out from the stem, it is the only example of its kind in the Algarve.

⑤ Casa da Cultura Islâmica e Mediterrânica

This space **(below)** in Largo de República promotes Silves' rich Islamic legacy and its links to Moorish and Mediterranean culture. It hosts art exhibitions and cultural events. For more details, contact the tourist office.

⑨ Igreja da Misericórdia

The highly decorative side doorway possibly served as the original entrance to the church **(left)** and shows the influence of the 16th-century Manueline style. The main chapel has a Renaissance altarpiece.

MOORISH SILVES

As Xelb, Silves was the capital of the Moorish province of al-Gharb, and by 1053 it had become a crowded metropolis. Writers, poets, scientists and philosophers lived here, and the shadows of several minarets fell across docks, a shipyard, public baths, a synagogue and a church. By the mid-12th century, however, Silves started to decline. Nonetheless, the legacy of 500 years of Moorish rule can still be seen in the local architecture and in the fields of orange, almond, fig and carob trees.

NEED TO KNOW

MAP F4

Tourist information: Parque das Merendes; (282) 098 927; open daily

Museu Municipal de Arqueologia: Rua das Portas de Loulé; 10am–6pm daily (last adm: 5:30pm); adm

Casa de Cultura Islâmica e Mediterránica: open only to groups

■ A pair of binoculars is useful when scanning the countryside from the castle ramparts.

■ The Café Inglês, just below the castle, is open daily for homemade fare. A rooftop terrace also operates here during the summer.

■ Pastelaria Dona Rosa, just off Rua 25 Abril, fronts a peaceful square, and is decorated with *azulejo* panels.

⑥ Arade River Cruises

The quay near the Roman bridge is where sightseeing boats from Portimão dock *(see p59)*. Look out for herons and flamingoes. Departure times depend on the tide.

⑦ Ponte Romana

Only the foundations of this very pretty whitewashed bridge date back to Roman times. The rest of the structure is medieval in origin. These days it is closed to traffic.

⑧ Quinta do Francês Vineyard

Set in a picturesque valley 6 km (4 miles) northwest of Silves, near Odeluca, this vineyard *(see p72)* offers guided tours and tastings of award-winning reds, whites and rosés.

⑩ Cruz de Portugal

Standing incongruously next to a main road, this exquisite 16th-century granite cross is said to have been a gift to the city from Dom Manuel I.

TOP 10 ⭐ Monchique

This pretty and engaging little market town nestles in the Serra de Monchique, a densely wooded canvas of eucalyptus, chestnut, pine and cork trees interrupted by tracts of barren moorland. A welcome change from beaches and villas, Monchique is all cobbled streets and rural sentiment. The local *medronho* – firewater distilled from the berries of the Arbutus (strawberry tree) – is the finest available anywhere.

1 Igreja Matriz

An intriguing Manueline doorway **(below)** greets visitors to Monchique's 16th-century parish church. The twisted columns resemble lengths of gnarled rope. Inside, the capitals of the columns in the three naves are similarly fashioned, suggesting a nautical theme.

2 Galeria de Santo António

This engaging art gallery, housed in a former 18th-century hermitage, hosts live music events as well as exhibitions featuring works by local and international artists.

3 Villa Termal das Caldas de Monchique Spa Resort

Set under a canopy of pine and eucalyptus, this modern thermal spa complex **(right)** retains a nostalgic air *(see p127)*.

The attractive market town of Monchique

4 Fóia

For the most stunning landscape views in the entire Algarve, head for the peak of Fóia. At 902 m (2,959 ft), this is the highest point in the Serra da Monchique. You can either drive or walk up along a well-marked path.

5 Barranco dos Pisões

A captivating little beauty and picnic spot in the woods about 4 km (2 miles) northwest of Monchique, the Barranco dos Pisões is known locally for its ancient water wheel and its 150-year-old plane tree.

Pedras Juntas
Pomba
Monchique
Alferce
392
267
Fóia
Celceira
267
Fornalha
Casais
267
Caldas de Monchique
Barracão
266

Monchique

5 6 1 2 9
4
3
10
8
7

6 Nossa Senhora do Desterro

A mysterious air pervades the ruins of the Franciscan monastery (above). Severely damaged by the 1755 earthquake, its empty shell echoes with the rustle of leaves from an immense magnolia tree standing in the old garden. The interior is closed to the public.

7 Parque da Mina

Centred around a disused iron-ore mine, this imaginative theme park (see p64) features a lovingly restored 18th-century manor house and a traditional distillery. There is also a playground and a nature trail, with picnic areas along the way.

8 Caldas de Monchique

The Romans were bowled over by this cosy hamlet in the Monchique hills, and totally impressed by the hot, curative properties of its waters (above).

MONCHIQUE'S SPA

According to legend, if you take a sip from the fountain of love, an ancient font hiding in the dappled woods behind Caldas de Monchique, you'll fall in love with life. The waters are said to be good for a whole host of maladies, including rheumatic and digestive disorders and skin complaints. The Romans certainly thought so, as did Dom João II. Today's visitors are offered a range of water-based therapies, using vapours, water jets, hydromassage, steam and hot algae.

9 Igreja de São Sebastião

The church (below) contains a beautifully sculpted 17th-century figure of Nossa Senhora do Desterro.

10 Picota

At 773 m (2,536 ft), the Algarve's second-highest peak doesn't quite command the same all-round vista as Fóia, but Picota is steeper and pleasantly wooded. Its location offers beautiful views that take in long sweeps of scented meadows and a sparkling, distant sea to the south.

NEED TO KNOW

MAP E3 ■ Visitor information: Largo S. Sebastião; (282) 911 189

Open Mon–Fri

Galeria de Santo António: Calçada de St. António; open only during special exhibitions and events

■ For a pleasant walk, follow the terraced footpath in the grounds of the spa complex.

■ Monchique is also known for its small wooden "scissor" chairs, which make good gifts.

■ Reasonably priced cafés and restaurants cluster round the central bus station.

■ Down in Caldas de Monchique, Café-Restaurante 1692 has a marvellous terrace that spills out onto the square, making it a good choice.

TOP 10 ⭐ Loulé

The pleasant inland town of Loulé is renowned for its traditional handicrafts and splendid market. The Romans first settled on the spot now occupied by the castle, but it was the Moors for whom Loulé was to become a place of some importance. Remnants of their presence can still be seen in the bell tower of Igreja Matriz de São Clemente, formerly a minaret. The castle is also Moorish in origin. Almonds and figs have been essential to the local economy for centuries.

Castelo ③

The ruins of this fortress underwent restoration during the 19th century, and today the castle **(right)** houses a museum *(see p45)*. Visitors are rewarded with grand views of the town from its battlements.

① Museu Municipal de Loulé

The highlight of this museum **(above)** is the first-floor recreation of a traditional Algarve kitchen, complete with 19th-century utensils and tableware *(see p47)*.

④ Pólo Museológico dos Frutos Secos

This original museum focuses on early harvesting methods for figs, carob and almond fruit. It was built in homage to a local businessman.

② Igreja Matriz de São Lourenço

About 8 km (5 miles) southeast of Loulé, at Almancil, blue and white *azulejo* panels grace the walls of the chancel, nave and the magnificent trompe-l'oeil cupola of this decorative church.

⑤ Ermida de Nossa Senhora da Conceição

This 16th-century chapel **(left)** is decorated with *azulejos* and has a stunning Baroque altarpiece. The ceiling panel is by the Loulé painter Rasquinho.

NEED TO KNOW

MAP J4 ■ Visitor Information: Ave 25 de Abril 9; (289) 463 900

Pólo Museológico dos Frutos Secos: Rua Gil Vincente 14

Loulé Carnival: in Feb (Shrove Tuesday)

Market: Praça da República; open 7am–3pm daily

Igreja Matriz de São Lourenço: **MAP J5**; Rua do Igreja, Almancil

■ When the Islamic bathhouse is closed, ask for the key at Rua Vice

Almirante Cândido dos Reis 36; (289) 400 642.

■ Rua de 5 Outubro has many bars, cafés and shops.

■ Order a *bica* (small coffee) at the historic Café Calcinha *(Praça da República 67)*.

6 Galeria de Arte do Convento do Espírito Santo

The decorated and vaulted ceilings of this former convent provide a splendid setting for the selection of contemporary paintings, sculptures and conceptual installations that are on display inside. There are regular contributions from local and international artists.

8 Igreja Matriz de São Clemente

Loulé's Muslim faithful were once summoned to prayer from the balcony of the lofty bell tower, which originally served as a minaret. Other highlights are the Capela de Nossa Senhora da Consolação and the Capela de São Brás's Baroque altarpiece.

TRADITIONAL CRAFTS

It was the inauguration of an artisans' fair back in 1291 that forged Loulé's reputation as a manufacturing centre. Many of the techniques used 800 years ago are still employed today. Ceramics are popular with tourists. In many local villages, residents still plait the leaves of dwarf palms to make hats, baskets and rugs; jute fibre is used to stitch pretty rag dolls. Saddleries tucked away in quiet hamlets supply harnesses for mules, and old wooden looms are used to produce shawls and blankets.

9 Banhos Islâmicos

The well-preserved ruins of an Islamic bathhouse known as *hammam de Al-'Ulyà* can be admired from a public viewing platform above the foundations, which date from the 1200s.

7 Loulé Carnival

The biggest, brightest and rowdiest of the Algarve's carnivals. Costume-clad revellers shake, rattle and roll for three days and nights to hybrid Latin rhythm and African-style percussion.

Loulé

8 km (5 miles)

10 Market

Mixed herbs, cheeses and red chilli peppers are sold alongside sweet figs, marzipan cakes and golden honey. Elsewhere, flowers, the freshest of fish, the ripest of fruit and a variety of genuine handicrafts **(above)**, make a visit to Loulé market an unforgettable shopping experience.

Following pages Panoramic view of Silves

Lagos

Lively, colourful and cheerful, Lagos is probably the most popular resort in the Algarve. Its easygoing atmosphere draws in a predominantly young crowd who are attracted to the bargain-stacked shops, the throng of bars and restaurants, some of the hippest nightlife on the south coast and the close proximity to lovely beaches and cliffs. Punctuating this cosmopolitan atmosphere is a rich historical vein – a source of great pride to the local population.

1 Igreja de Santo António

This 18th-century church is a jewel in the Algarve crown. Its gilded and painted woodwork over-flows with opulence. Everything the Baroque age is famous for is here: double-chinned cherubs, mythical beasts and ripened fruit. Entry is via the Museu Municipal Dr José Formosinho.

3 Forte da Ponta da Bandeira

Accessible via a drawbridge, this 17th-century fortress **(above)** was built to defend the harbour. Its ramparts now protect a small museum dedicated to the Age of Discoveries.

4 Ponta da Piedade

Parts of the dramatic headland **(below)**, 3 km (2 miles) northwest of the town, resemble a huge wedge of crumbling ginger cake. Beneath gnarled sandstone cliffs, towering outcrops of umber-hued rock rise up, hiding a warren of caves and grottoes. The lighthouse is a prime spot from which to watch the sunset.

5 Museu Municipal Dr José Formosinho

This museum houses an extra-ordinary collection of artifacts and oddities, plus one or two national treasures *(see pp28–9)*. Of note are the Roman mosaics and a collection of intricately carved and hand-painted model fishing boats.

2 Igreja de Santa Maria

The town's parish church **(above)** dates back to the 16th century, although much of what you see today was rebuilt in the 19th century. The church, however, still retains its Renaissance doorway with Doric columns and busts of São Pedro (St Peter) and São Paulo (St Paul) on either side of the archivolt.

7 Marina de Lagos

With 462 pontoon berths for yachts up to 30 m (100 ft) long, this first-class marina **(left)** enjoys an international reputation. Distinguished with several awards, including a European Blue Flag, it is also known for its bars, restaurants and cafés. Several coastal- and river-cruise companies are based here.

10 Praia do Camilo

A long wooden staircase leads down to this delightful wedge of golden sand, hemmed in by a series of ornate rock formations in rich ochre tones. Craggy stacks, the colour of gingerbread, rise out of the shallows and create a natural shelter against the wind. Countless seabirds find shelter here.

Slave Market Site 8

The northeastern corner of Praça Infante Dom Henrique **(right)** was the site of Europe's first slave market in the 15th century.

400 m (430 yards) 🚌 7 **600 m (650 yards)**
800 m (870 yards) 🚉 9 **5 km (3 miles)**

R. CAMACHINHOS
RUA C. JOAQUIM MACHADO
R. DR. F. SILVA
RUA DAS PORTAS DE PORTUGAL
JA DR. JOSÉ ALMEIDA
PRAÇA GIL EANES
AVENIDA DOS
PRAÇA LUÍS DE CAMÕES
i
RUA DA ALMEIDA
RUA DA BARROCA
RUA 25 DE ABRIL
GRES
R. 1.° DE MAIO
R. LARANJEIRA
RUA MARREIROS NETO
RUA DA EXTREMA
RUA DR. J. TELO
RUA 1.° DE MAIO
DESCOBRIMENTOS
JA DE FERRADURA
RUA CANDIDO DOS REIS
SOEIRA DA COSTA
RUA DA SILVA LOPES
JA LUÍS DE AZEVEDO
8
PRAÇA INFANTE D. HENRIQUE
2
RUA DO CASTELO DOS GOVERNADORES
RUA DE GIL VICENTE
PR. DA REPÚBLICA
1
5
RUA LANCAROTE DE FREITAS
RUA CARDEAL NETO
TR. DO FORNO
RUA 5 DE OUTUBRO
RUA 1.° DE MENDONÇA
R. GEN. ALBERTO SILVEIRA
R. DO JARDIM
RUA DR. JÚLIO DANTAS
3
RUA DR. R. MIGUEL BOMBARDA
RUA DA PORTA DA VILA
2.5 km (1 mile) 10
3 km (2 miles) 4 ↓

0 metres   100
0 yards   100

6 Town Walls

The foundations of the town walls date from Roman times, and were strengthened during Arab and Christian occupation. Restored in the 16th century, the best-preserved section encases a Manueline window from which Dom Sebastião *(see p29)* is said to have addressed townsfolk before going to Alcácer Quibir.

9 Monte da Casteleja Organic Farm and Vineyard

This charming estate promotes organic farming and produces fine wine. Just 4 km (2 miles) east of the city centre, the winery *(see p73)* sits in stunning rolling countryside, where a traditional farmhouse serves as a wine-tasting centre.

NEED TO KNOW

MAP D5 ■ Tourist office: Praça Gil Eanes; (282) 763 031

Museu Municipal Dr José Formosinho: Rua General Alberto Silveira; open 10am–12:30pm & 2–5:30pm Tue–Sun; adm

■ For a boat trip to the grottoes, embark from Avenida dos Descobrimentos, in front of the marina. On this route you will pass Dona Ana beach.

■ Cafés, bars and restaurants along the Frente Ribeirinha esplanade provide appetizing drinks and meals, as well as harbour-front views.

■ For almond delicacies and Italian ice cream, visit Taquelim Gonçalves on the marina.

Highlights of Lagos Museu Municipal Dr José Formosinho

The extravagant Baroque altar at Igreja de Santo António

1 Igreja de Santo António

After visiting the museum, it is worth taking time to appreciate the adjacent church. The opulent 18th-century interior, with its spectacular excess of gilded Baroque carvings, *azulejo* panels and decorated ceiling, is extravagant and impressive, and its finery is a compelling sight.

2 Senhora do Forte Model Village

Housed in the Ethnographic Hall is a remarkable labour of love: a huge scale model of an imaginary Algarve coastal town. Constructed with breathtaking attention to detail,

Model of an imaginary Algarve village

it took Lagos resident Pedro Reis 5,300 hours to build over a three-year, seven-month period.

3 Traditional Portuguese Boats

This impressive collection of 28 miniature boats was skilfully carved out of wood and hand-painted by local artisan, Arez Viegas. The models include barges, launches, fishing boats and steamers. The prize exhibit is the frigate, *D. Fernando II e Glória*.

4 Altar de Campanha

An extraordinary 17th-century mobile altar that was carried by Portuguese troops into the field and used for prayer between military engagements. A carved statue of St Anthony rests on top of the altar, which is inlaid with gold leaf.

5 São Gonçalo de Lagos

A delightful anomaly, the 18th-century statue of Lagos' patron saint is incorporated into the door of a cupboard that was used by the priests of the time to store their robes.

6 Priests' Vestments

A number of fine examples of priests' vestments are displayed in the Sacred Art wing of the museum, but the most outstanding garment is the one worn at a Mass attended by King Dom Sebastião I soon before his death. The crusading king perished on the Moroccan battlefield along with 8,000 of his troops in 1578. The robe is hand-embroidered with gold.

7 Foral Dado a Lagos (Town Charter)

Presented to Lagos by Dom Manuel I in 1504, the facsimile on display is of the opening page of the rare manuscript, embossed with gold leaf.

The beautifully illustrated Foral Dado

8 Portrait of Estevão Amarante

The life-sized portrait (not always on display) of the late Portuguese thespian, Estevão Amarante, is by Fernando Santos. As you walk past the image, the change in perspective appears to make Sr Amarante's left foot move with you – a very eerie sensation.

9 Cork Altarpiece

A masterpiece of cork whittling, this framed, three-dimensional retable was carved by Silves resident, Francisco Figueiras in 1907. Its filigree decoration is extremely delicate.

STORY OF LAGOS

Lagos has "welcomed" visitors ever since the Phoenicians and Carthaginians established settlements along the banks of its superb natural harbour more than 2,000 years ago. Under subsequent Roman occupation, the town became known as Lacobriga, and flourished as a busy trading port. The ever-cautious Moors built a double ring of ramparts around its centre during their occupation of the area, but that was not enough to repel the Christians who conquered the city in 1241.

During the 15th century – the period of Portugal's Golden Age of Discoveries – Henry the Navigator's caravels departed Lagos shipyards bound for far-flung African regions, and the town quickly became a centre for trade in ivory, gold, silver and other exotic merchandise. Unfortunately, a far more unsavoury enterprise was also spawned: slavery.

Lagos became the capital of the Algarve in 1576 and remained so until 1756, when the honour was transferred first to Tavira, and then finally to Faro. By that time, however, much of the Algarve, Lagos included, lay in ruins after the devastating **1755** earthquake, a fact that seems unimaginable today.

10 Opus Vermiculatum Mosaic

This impressive, near-complete Roman mosaic was unearthed in 1933 by the museum's founder, Dr José Formosinho, near Budens, around 10 km (6 miles) west of Lagos. Complementing it is a smaller but wholly intact example discovered at Abicada, 2 km (1 mile) east of Portimão.

TOP 10 ★ Parque Natural da Ria Formosa

The Parque Natural da Ria Formosa comprises an extensive lagoon that follows 60 km (37 miles) of coastline between Manta Rota and Vale do Lobo. Made up of sand-dune islands, marshland, saltpans and freshwater lakes, the habitat provides sanctuary for an astonishing assortment of flora and fauna, including birds such as white storks and the rare purple gallinule. The park's headquarters are located at Quinta de Marim, 3 km (2 miles) east of Olhão.

1 Quinta do Lago Nature Trail

This partly shaded trail highlights the flora of two widely differing ecosystems: woodland and salt marshland. The path winds past umbrella and maritime pines.

Aerial view of Parque Natural da Ria Formosa

2 São Lourenço Nature Trail

One of the most rewarding introductions to the reserve is to follow the 3-km (2-mile) São Lourenço nature trail (**above**). It will bring you into close contact with two different types of wetland: the salt marshes and the freshwater lagoons.

3 Roman Salting Tanks

Five Roman salting tanks (**right**) can be explored near the freshwater lagoons. Dating from the 2nd century AD, they were once used for salting fish prior to their distribution all over Rome's empire.

4 Recuperation Centre for Animals

This hospital and rehabilitation centre for sick and injured animals has an area where visitors can obtain more information about the Algarve's wildlife and the animals being treated here.

5 Tide Mill

Tide mills were once very common in the lagoon and estuaries along the Portuguese coastline. Power was obtained by utilizing the change in water levels associated with shifting tides. The example on the Ria Formosa **(right)** is the last of 30 that used to operate.

7 Freshwater Lagoons and Hides

The freshwater lagoons provide vital refuge for nesting and migrating birds, and harbour a miscellany of aquatic mammals. The views from the observation hides bring this sparkling marine oasis into sharp focus.

8 Olhão Nature Trail

The longest trail in the reserve meanders past a tide mill, the remains of Roman salting tanks and several wildlife observation hides before looping back to the park's headquarters.

9 Ecoteca Museu João Lúcio

João Lúcio, 19th-century poet, lawyer and former mayor of Olhão, owned much of the land on which Quinta de Marim is now situated. His former villa, near the river's edge, is now an ecomuseum.

10 Coastal Conifer Woods

Coastal conifer woodland is sparse in the eastern Algarve, but where it occurs it provides an efficient means of coastal protection and adds to the diverse beauty of the terrain.

NEED TO KNOW

MAP K–L6 ■ Park headquarters: Quinta de Marim; call (289) 700 210 for information about volunteering and conservation projects

Park: open 9am–8pm Mon–Fri, 10am–6:30pm Sat & Sun (winter: to 5:30pm)

Ecoteca Museu João Lúcio: (289) 700 940; open 9am–12:30pm & 2–5:30pm Mon–Fri

....

■ It is advisable to wear a pair of sturdy walking boots if you are planning to follow the nature trails. You will need to put on warm clothing in winter.

■ Photographers in the hides will need a telephoto lens of at least 300 mm.

■ The Vista Formosa restaurant opposite the park's main entrance serves a good selection of fresh grilled fish.

6 Coastal Dunes

The sweeping tracts of sand **(below)** guarding the mouth of the estuary constitute a fragile environment, partly held together by the vegetation that has colonized them.

Wildlife of the Ria Formosa

Purple gallinule by the lagoon

1 Purple Gallinule
Very rare, this striking bird is reclusive in nature and tends to play hide-and-seek in the cattail that sprouts along the edge of the freshwater lagoons. A dark-coloured relative of the moorhen, there are numerous couples in residence.

2 Kentish Plover
Found at large along the eastern Algarve coastline, this small wading bird is a talented actor. If you stray too close to its nesting site, it will drag one wing along the ground as if it has been injured, to lure intruders away from its young.

3 Mediterranean Chameleon
This is a treat indeed for anyone lucky enough to spy one of these remarkable creatures, with its colour-coordinated skin. Hibernating from December to March, the best time to see this bulbous-eyed reptile out and about is on early spring mornings.

4 European Pond Terrapin
A whimsical little member of the chelonian family, this diminutive amphibian is fond of lakes, ponds and calm rivers. It is usually only detected as it darts for shelter at the sound of approaching feet. Tread lightly when you are on the look-out for these creatures.

5 Azure-Winged Magpie
A handsome, cheeky bird frequently heard chattering in small groups among the pinewoods near Quinta do Lago. Easily recognizable by its sooty crown and nape, the blue flash of its wing feathers makes this species particularly alluring in flight.

6 Viperine Snake
The great pretender, this snake is distinguished by its zigzag dorsal line and chestnut-coloured scales, which imitate those of a viper. If disturbed it will rear up, inflate its neck and spit. However, it is all theatrics – the snake is completely harmless.

Hoopoe

7 Hoopoe
An exotic-looking bird with a lovely salmon-pink crest, the hoopoe is the golfer's companion, often seen probing for cutworm on the manicured grass of fairways across the Algarve. Primarily a summer visitor, some individuals remain in the region throughout the winter.

8 Greater Flamingo
There is not a sight more majestic than a band of flamingoes panning for food on the salinas. Large flocks of these graceful birds gather in the park

Greater flamingo

during autumn, en route to winter breeding grounds, but they can also be spotted in the summer.

9 Little Tern

The little tern's favoured nesting site in Portugal is along the Ria Formosa, but the fact that it nests on the sand means that breeding is, at best, precarious.

10 Fiddler Crab

Often seen scuttling in panic across the mud at low tide, the male of the species has one of its pincers (left or right) considerably more developed than the other. Its European distribution is confined wholly to the Iberian peninsula.

The distinctive fiddler crab

PRESERVING THE ENVIRONMENT

For those visitors who want to spend more time at the wonderful Ria Formosa and help to preserve and conserve its varied wildlife, the Centro de Educação Ambiental de Marim (Marim Environmental Educational Centre – CEAM) works to protect the environment and promote a balanced, sustainable development of the park's natural resources. It runs a number of projects manned by volunteers, and members of the public are welcome to join in its efforts. Assisting at the Wildlife Recovery Centre, where sick and injured wild birds and animals are nurtured back to health, is one of the most popular programmes. There is a waiting list to join the team of volunteers, and those interested in this, or any of CEAM's other projects, should call (289) 700 210 or check www.natural.pt.

TOP 10 PLANTS IN THE PARK

Dunes

1 Marram grass (helps to support the dune)

2 Sea holly (top of dune)

3 Thrift (centre of dune)

4 Sea daffodil (delicate white flowers in summer)

Coastal Woodland

5 Furze (thorny shrub)

Salt Marsh

6 Cord grass (endures long submersion)

7 Sea lavender (identified by spikes of white, pink or mauve flowers)

8 Sea purslane (lance-shaped leaves and purple flowers)

Freshwater Lagoon

9 Cattail (cylindrical spike)

10 Rush (ideal shelter for aquatic wildlife)

The salt marshes and lagoons of the Parque Natural da Ria Formosa are a haven for a wide variety of flora and fauna.

TOP 10 ⭐ Sagres

In summer, this small harbour town overflows with youngsters armed with surfboards and a *joie de vivre*. Crammed with welcoming *pensões*, it is an excellent base from which to explore the fine beaches spread along the Algarve's untamed west coast. Sagres is the most southwesterly community in continental Europe, and its lively atmosphere is infectious.

1 Fortaleza de Santo António de Beliche

Perched on a pinnacle overlooking the Atlantic Ocean, this 17th-century fortification **(below)** also contains a small chapel, which in turn marks the site of an even earlier ruined church.

Sagres

2 Menhir Circuit

Starting near Hortas do Tabual, this 2 km (1 mile) circular walk passes a series of *menhirs*, or megaliths – monumental stones that date back to 3000 BC.

3 Nossa Senhora da Graça

The foundations of this graceful 16th-century chapel, facing Cabo de São Vicente, are said to have been laid by Prince Henry the Navigator.

Cabo de São Vicente (4)

The forbidding look of this windblown cape **(right)** is quite awe-inspiring *(see p100)*. Greek historian Strabo, writing at the time of Christ, believed it to be the end "of all the inhabited earth".

(7) Farol do Cabo de São Vicente

The tidy buildings around this lighthouse *(farol)* incorporate a small museum, snack bar and gift shop. The tower is closed to the public but the fortifications offer majestic views of the coastline.

(5) Parque Natural do Sudoeste Alentejano e Costa Vicentina

This wild and beautiful park **(above)** covers nearly all of the western coast of the Algarve *(see p100)*. It protects a complex ecosystem and lies under a busy migratory flight path for birds.

(8) Forte da Baleeira

A crumbling wall and arch are virtually all that remain of the harbour fortification, but the coastal view from the headland is superb.

(6) Fortaleza de Sagres

Ominous, stark and, in its time, virtually impregnable, two solid bastions and massive front walls are the impressive hallmarks of this 18th-century fort *(see p45)*. Little else resembles a defensive structure today, except perhaps the mighty cliffs themselves.

HENRY THE NAVIGATOR (1394–1460)

A brooding, scholarly and devout man, Prince Henry brought together the most learned of astron-omers and astrologers, skilled cartographers and geographers, and the very best boat designers, to create a school of naviga-tion known as Vila do Infante. He oversaw and sponsored many a perilous expedition, and his vision and dedication eventually mapped the way for Portugal's Golden Age of Discoveries.

(10) Ponta de Sagres Panoramic Walk

A bracing walk can be enjoyed around the edge of the promontory. Next to the lighthouse is a vast blowhole where you can hear the pounding of the ocean as it crashes into the rocks far below.

(9) Rosa dos Ventos

The extraordinary giant wind rose, or wind compass – a device used for measuring the direction of the wind – is said to have been built for Prince Henry the Navigator, although it may actually date from the 16th century. It is an impressive 43 m (141 ft) in diameter. The intriguing circle and its radiating points have been marked by pebbles **(above)**.

TOP 10 ⭐ Albufeira

Albufeira is one of Portugal's most popular holiday destinations and the largest resort in the Algarve. Famed for its fabulous beaches and nightlife, the town gets very busy in summer, when it positively bursts with energy. Its history is just as animated, from Roman settlement 2,000 years ago, Arab and Christian conquest in the 8th and 13th centuries respectively, to its rise and fall as a centre of trade and the emergence of its fishing industry.

5 Galeria Pintor Samora Barros

Named in honour of the artist/poet whose diligent handiwork adorns the parish church in Albufeira, this airy gallery overlooking the town square stages work by contemporary Portuguese and international artists.

1 Praia dos Pescadores

"Beach of the Fishermen" **(above)** is so named because of the many fishing vessels left on the sand between use. The grizzled fishermen who own the boats seem oblivious to the sunbathers who descend on this well-known beach in summer.

2 Castle Walls

The mighty ramparts that once surrounded Albufeira crumbled to dust as the 1755 earthquake struck. A corner wall, the North Door, does survive though, in Rua Joaquim Pedro Samora. A remnant of St Anne's Gate also still stands, which forms part of a restaurant interior today.

4 Museu Municipal de Arqueologia

Peer closely and you'll spy some charming exhibits **(below)** at this museum. Highlights include Roman earrings and a 7th-century Visigoth earthenware wine goblet (see p47).

3 Igreja de São Sebastião

The altarpiece is the shining star of this exquisite church. Its gilded form presides over a 14th-century statue of Nossa Senhora da Orada, who is shown clutching a baby Jesus.

7 Adega do Cantor

Owned by British singer Sir Cliff Richard, this vineyard **(left)** lies 6 km (4 miles) northwest of Albufeira, behind the Algarve Shopping mall *(see p74)*. Pre-booked guided tours include tastings *(see p72)*, which are held in the well-stocked shop.

6 Marina de Albufeira

The marina **(below)**, located 4 km (2 miles) west of the resort, is the departure point for sightseeing cruises, diving expeditions and fishing excursions. It is also home to a number of good bars and restaurants.

8 Parque Aventura

The Adventure Park features high-rope obstacle courses for a range of age groups (starting at the age of four), set at varied heights within the trees. There is also a paintball area.

WATERSPORTS

The crystal-clear waters of the Atlantic provide the Algarve with a thriving watersports scene. Fun begins with the humble pedalo, but for the more sea-hardy a diving centre (www.easydivers.pt) at Marina de Albufeira is great for beginners. For kids, the Leãozinho pirate ship (www. dreamwave algarve.com) explores the nearby grottoes. Praia da Galé, about 6 km (4 miles) west, is known for its jet- and water-skiing, while windsurfers and paragliders head for Praia da Falésia.

---

9 Praia da Oura

 Albufeira's "Golden Beach" fringes the village-resort of the same name, giving it the advantage of proximity to shops and cafés.

10 "The Strip"

 Glitzy, gaudy and totally irresistible, this is Albufeira's mini Las Vegas: a narrow, neon-lit runway of hotels and restaurants, pubs, cafés and DJ-bars, with the odd *artesanato* (craft shop) squeezed in. Two of the region's top nightclubs, Kiss and Libertos, are found here.

NEED TO KNOW

MAP G5 ■ Tourist information office: Rua 5 de Outubro 8; (289) 585 279

Parque Aventura: (913) 185 782; open mid-Jun–mid-Sep: 10am–6pm daily; mid-Sep–mid-Jun: 2–6pm daily.

■ Albufeira bus station is 2 km (1 mile) north of the old town. Almost all buses from the resort arrive or depart from here. Visit www.algarvebus.info for more details on facilities and timetables *(see p117)*.

■ Albufeira is awash with bars and cafés, but those lining Largo Cais Herculano are particularly appealing. Try Cabana Fresca, right in front of Praia dos Pescadores, known for its tasty seafood snacks.

TOP10 ⭐ **Portimão**

Once the centre of the region's fishing industry, Portimão is better known today as a vibrant tourism hub. The old town's 18th-century veneer, the landscaped riverfront and several highly regarded visitor attractions help to showcase this busy port. Leisure options, meanwhile, extend to a fabulous beach, an international marina and a fascinating offshore diving site.

1 Marina de Portimão

At the mouth of the Rio Arade, the marina **(above)** provides 620 pontoon berths for watercraft up to 50 m (165 ft). Shops, restaurants and bars line the boardwalk near the beach.

3 Teatro Municipal de Portimão

This first-class performing arts venue stages regular music concerts, theatre productions and contemporary dance acts. There is also a lively café upstairs.

4 Monumentos Megalíticos de Alcalar

One of the region's most important archaeological sites lies 10 km (6 miles) away at Alcalar. A 5,000-year-old megalithic burial chamber is the main sight.

6 Quinta do Morgado da Torre

Guided tours of the winery (see p73) followed by tastings can be booked at this highly regarded vineyard, situated 7 km (4 miles) northwest of the city centre. Wines produced here include Tapada da Torre Reserva.

5 Autódromo Internacional do Algarve

Prestigious motorsport tournaments and a classic-car festival (see p76) are hosted at this racetrack **(below)**, 15 km (9 miles) north of Portimão.

2 Museu de Portimão

Occupying a former cannery, this award-winning museum **(above)** traces the town's prehistoric, Roman and Islamic heritage (see p47). Its fish-canning industry is also explored.

7 Praia da Rocha

Praia da Rocha **(below)** is named after its beach *(see p49)*, one of the most impressive in the Algarve. The resort's plethora of hotels, nightclubs and restaurants is a magnet for Portimão residents and holiday-makers.

8 Ocean Revival Park

Submerged 4 km (2 miles) off the coast are four decommissioned navy vessels sunk to create a fascinating artificial reef. You can explore the site through diving centres certified by the park *(see p82)*.

MARITIME HERITAGE

Portimão's history is bound up with the river and the sea. The Romans settled here for the Arade Waterway, a valuable gateway between the Mediterranean and the Atlantic. In the modern era, a prosperous fishing and canning industry developed. Inevitably, the passage of time saw fish stocks depleted and factories closed down. The tide turned, however, with the rise in tourism. Today, a fleet of sightseeing boats navigate the estuary, and the town welcomes cruise liners from around the world.

10 Igreja do Antigo Colégio da Companhia de Jesus

The imposing pyramid-like façade of this remarkable 17th-century structure provides the old town with a unique architectural reference point. The interior features Baroque altarpieces and the tomb of Diogo Gonçalves, the church's founder.

9 Igreja de Nossa Senhora da Conceição

Little is left of the original church **(left)**, destroyed in the 1755 earthquake *(see p43)*. The portico, however, survived and remains a fine example of 15th-century architecture.

NEED TO KNOW

MAP E4 ■ Visitor information: Teatro Municipal de Portimão, Largo 1º de Dezembro; (282) 402 487; open 9:30am–5:30pm Mon–Fri

Teatro Municipal de Portimão: Largo 1º de Dezembro; open Tue–Sat

Museu de Portimão: Rua D. Carlos I; (282) 405 230; open Aug: 3–11pm Wed–Sun, 7:30–11pm Tue; Sep–Jul: 10am–6pm Wed–Sun, 2:30–6pm Tue; adm

Igreja do Antigo Colégio da Companhia de Jesus: open 8am–12:30pm & 3:30–5:30pm Mon–Fri

Monumentos Magalíticos de Alcalar: **MAP E5**; Mexilhoeira Grande; (282) 471 410; open Aug: 10am–1pm & 2–6pm Tue–Sat; Sep–July: 10am–1pm & 2–4:30pm Tue–Sat; adm

■ Sightseeing cruises along the Rio Arade and to the coast depart from the esplanade *(see p59)*.

■ The 17th-century Fortaleza da Santa Catarina, at the eastern end of Praia da Rocha, offers fine views.

■ For a romantic dinner, book a table at Vista Restaurant *(Avenida Tomás Cabreira, Praia da Rocha; www.vista restaurante.com)*.

The Top 10 of Everything

FIESA International Sand Sculpture Festival

🔟 Moments in History

1 **3000 BC: Early People and Trade**
Stone burial chambers (dolmens) and menhirs are characteristic of this period. By 1000 BC, the Phoenicians had established sizeable trading stations. The Greeks also arrived, but their trade links were severed by the Carthaginians, who blockaded the Straits of Gibraltar, and in 550 BC founded the city of Portus Hannibalis (Portimão).

Menhir dating from c.3000 BC

2 **218–201 BC: Second Punic War**
The Romans defeated the Carthaginians, then swept through the Iberian peninsula. During the next 400 years, grand Roman cities and luxurious villas developed.

3 **AD 415: Visigoths**
After the fall of the Roman Empire, the reins of power were seized by the Visigoths, a formidable warrior caste that came from eastern France and Germany.

4 **711: Arrival of the Moors**
Internal strife and persecution among the Visigoths ultimately led to one faction appealing for aid from Muslim North Africa. A large army of Berbers and Arabs conquered huge swathes of the Iberian peninsula. The Moors dominated the Algarve for more than 500 years, giving the region its name, al-Gharb, and turning Silves into an intellectual hub of staggering opulence.

5 **Christian Crusades**
Though Christians reconquered central Portugal in the 12th century, the Algarve was still firmly under Moorish rule. Dom Sancho (1185–1212) briefly took Silves in 1189, but the city was recaptured by Al-Mansur. Dom Sancho II (1223–48) later launched a campaign to invade southern Portugal with the help of northern European Crusaders.

6 **Portugal is Born**
Faro was the last Moorish stronghold to fall in 1249. Portuguese sovereignty over the Algarve was confirmed in a treaty with the kingdom of Castile in 1297.

7 **Era of the Great Discoveries**
The Algarve played a pivotal role in Portugal's maritime expansion in the 15th century. Henry the Navigator was made governor of the Algarve in 1418 and initiated the voyages of discovery from his bases in Sagres and Lagos. By the time of his death in 1460, Madeira, the Azores and Cape Verde islands had been discovered and much of the west coast of Africa had been mapped. In 1488 Bartolomeu Dias discovered the Cape of Good Hope, and later Vasco da Gama opened the trade route to India.

Painting of Henry the Navigator

Portrait of Portuguese ruler João V

8 Artistic Extravagance
The discovery of gold and diamonds in Brazil during the reign of Pedro II (1683–1706) later financed a period of great artistic extravagance under João V, who ruled Portugal until 1750.

9 Great Earthquake of 1755
The earthquake of 1755 devastated Lisbon and much of southern Portugal and plunged the nation into a long-lasting crisis. Napoleon's troops later invaded in 1807.

Salazar's military coup, 1974

10 Republicanism and Integration with Europe
The late 19th century witnessed political strife, with Republicanism taking root. António de Oliveira Salazar became prime minister in 1932, and turned around a stagnating economy but with the sacrifice of democracy. The army overthrew the government in 1974 in a near-bloodless coup. On 1 January 2002, the country adopted the euro.

MYTHS AND LEGENDS

1 The Moorish King and the Nordic Princess
The mythical king planted thousands of almond trees to convince the princess that the blossom was like the snow she was used to.

2 Henry the Navigator
Henry assembled the best nautical minds in an academy which, however, has left no physical trace.

3 Curse of the Vixen
On stormy nights, the bellows of a beast can be heard in the hinterland.

4 The Cry of Aben Afen
Listen out for battle cries near Silves – the ghost of the city's last Arab lord.

5 St Vincent
Cabo de São Vicente is associated with a 4th-century martyr, whose body was watched over by 10 ravens.

6 Enchanted Cássima
The pitiful cries of a Moorish woman supposedly echo in the streets close to Loulé Castle.

7 Hannibal and the Elephants
Legend has it that the great general landed with his troops at Portimão.

8 Manueline Window
King Dom Sebastião (1557–78) is said to have roused an army from the window at Lagos Castle.

9 Pot of Treasure
A pot full of gold coins lies on the road between Mexilhoeira Grande and Praia da Rocha. Kiss the toad guarding it, and the pot is yours.

10 Capture of Aljezur Castle, 1249
A maid might have prevented the capture, but mistook the attacking knights for Moorish defenders and failed to raise the alarm.

Aljezur Castle, captured in 1249

TOP 10 Castles and Forts

of the original structure. Inside, the chapel of Nossa Senhora da Assunção lies in mournful pieces.

3 Salir
MAP J3

The ruins of Salir's Moorish castle have been put to novel effect by locals who have sunk gardens in between the battlements and the keep. The rest of the structure can be explored by treading a circular path around the middle of the fortifications. An interesting museum (see p47) completes the picture.

The battlements of Silves Castle

1 Silves
MAP F4 ■ Open 9am–5:30pm daily (summer: to 7pm) ■ Adm

One of the Algarve's great landmarks, well-preserved Silves Castle dates back to Moorish times, but may have been built on Roman fortifications. Its formidable red sandstone battlements and massive polygonal towers enclose a vast compound.

2 Paderne
MAP G4

The atmospheric ruins of Paderne's long-abandoned Moorish castle are best appreciated on a Sunday morning, or an early evening when the ramparts are illuminated. The thick outer walls of mud and sandstone and the remains of a barbican tower are all that exist

4 Alcoutim

Enjoying a lovely setting, Alcoutim (see p91) commands glorious views across the River Guadiana to the neighbouring Spanish town of Sanlúcar. The inhabitants of the two settlements were once enemies, but the 14th-century castle was where the short-lived peace treaty between Fernando I and Henrique of Castile was signed on 31 March 1371.

5 Aljezur
MAP C3

Dominating the landscape around Aljezur (see p101) are the ruins of the town's 10th-century castle. Perched on a hillock with

Statue of a smuggler, Alcoutim

fabulous views of the coast and Serra de Monchique, this Moorish stronghold controlled an ancient river port and provided a vital link with the open sea. Its broad, overgrown courtyard hides remnants of a vaulted cistern and is surrounded by high ramparts, reinforced by two towers – one round, the other square.

6 Tavira
MAP M4 ■ Open summer: 8:30am–7pm Mon–Fri, 10am–7pm Sat & Sun; winter: 8:30am–5pm Mon–Fri, 9am–5pm Sat & Sun

Only the walls of this old Moorish fortification remain, which surrounds a charming, well-maintained garden. There are lovely views.

7 Fortaleza de Cacela Velha
MAP N4 ■ Closed to public

This pocket-sized fortress sits in the quaint hamlet of Cacela Velha, 8 km (5 miles) west of Monte Gordo, in the eastern Algarve. Polygonal in shape, the building dates from the 18th century and enjoys commanding views over a lagoon that teems with waterfowl. Its squat turrets are topped with whitewashed cones.

8 Fortaleza de Sagres
The fortress is steeped in history and myth, with huge walls and bastions dating from 1793. Little, if anything, remains of Henry the Navigator's original fortress (see p35). Whether or not there was an academy of navigation and astronomy founded here remains

a matter of debate and legend. An 18th-century sundial fashioned into the wall is aligned with the famous wind compass, the Rosa dos Ventos.

The view from Fortaleza de Sagres

9 Loulé
MAP J4 ■ Open 9am–6pm Mon–Fri, 9am–2pm Sat ■ Adm

Standing on a site (see pp22–3) first occupied by the Romans and later by the Moors, the restored battlements here offer splendid views from the ramparts. Dom Afonso III (1210–79) strengthened and expanded the walls of what was a modest military fortification before adding towers and a keep to create a castle.

10 Castelo de Castro Marim
MAP P3 ■ Open Apr–Oct: 9am–7pm daily; Nov–Mar: 9am–5pm ■ Adm

The colossal frontier castle of Castro Marim overlooks the border between Spain and Portugal. Built in the 13th century, the castle was the first headquarters of the Order of Christ. Henry the Navigator was a frequent visitor.

Castelo de Castro Marim

🔟 Museums

① Museu Municipal Dr José Formosinho

This highly entertaining ethnographic museum brings together a fantastic collection of oddities, rarities and priceless treasures *(see pp26–9)*.

Museu Municipal Dr José Formosinho

② Museu Municipal de Arqueologia, Silves

This excellent museum *(see pp18–19)* is unique in Portugal for its astonishing 12th-century Arab well-cistern. Unearthed by chance in 1980, it is the star exhibit around which the entire building is constructed. An original staircase, closed to the public and incorporated into the ancient structure, descends 15 m (49 ft) to the bottom of the well. The museum also displays a range of prehistoric, Roman and Moorish antiquities found in Silves.

③ Museu Cerro da Vila, Vilamoura

MAP H5 ■ Cerro da Vila
■ Open May–Oct: 10am–1pm & 4–9pm daily; Nov–Apr: 9:30am– 12:30pm & 2–6pm daily ■ Adm

A first-rate modern museum and historic Roman site, Cerro da Vila in Vilamoura is an outstanding example of a 2nd-century villa complex, with sunken baths, salt tanks, a burial tower and brilliant black-and-white-patterned mosaics. The adjacent museum houses a superb display of Roman, Visigoth and Moorish artifacts.

④ Nucleo Islâmico, Tavira

The interior of this absorbing museum *(see pp16–7)* is built around a 12th-century Islamic wall. Among its various exhibits include an inkwell that dates back to the 13th century. There is also a rare eight-handle ceramic pan from the same period. The extraordinary 11th-century "Tavira Vase" is the standout piece.

⑤ Museu Municipal de Faro

Set within the cloisters of the former convent of Nossa Senhora da Assunção, this museum is one of the Algarve's most beautiful *(see pp12–13)*. It contains a large collection of artifacts and tells the story of Faro's development from Roman times to the present day. Highlights include a giant Roman floor mosaic, fragments of a large Moorish bowl inscribed with "Allah" and a gallery devoted to 16th-century Italian, Spanish and Portuguese paintings.

Museu Municipal de Faro

Exhibit in the Museu de Portimão

6 Museu de Portimão

This superb museum (see pp38–9) charts the development of the region's local communities, in particular the fish-canning industry, a former mainstay of the Portuguese economy. Housed in what was once a sardine-canning factory, the museum contains many of the machines used in the industry, and details the processes involved. Other highlights include Roman and Moorish artifacts and the factory's former 19th-century cistern.

7 Museu Municipal de Arqueologia, Albufeira

MAP G5 ■ 1 Praça da República, Albufeira ■ Open 9:30am–12:30pm & 1:30–5:30pm Tue, Sat & Sun, 9:30am–5:30pm Wed, 9:30am–5:30pm Thu & Fri (Jul–Aug: 2–10pm Thu & Fri) ■ Adm

Looking out over the ocean, this modern museum in Albufeira houses a modest but fascinating collection of Stone Age, Roman and Moorish artifacts. The 10th-century Arab silo is worth close scrutiny, as is the set of weathered 16th-century keystones.

8 Pólo Museológico de Salir, Salir

MAP J3 ■ Largo Pedro Dias, Salir ■ (289) 489 137 ■ Open 9am–1pm & 2–5pm Mon–Fri

This museum, housed in the ruins of Salir's Moorish castle (see pp44–5), showcases glazed ceramic bottles and pots dating from the 12th century. Artifacts also include a silver dirham and a funeral tablet inscribed in Arabic. The museum's glass floor is set over an excavated street and remains of dwellings from the time of Islamic occupation. An outdoor platform offers views of the castle walls.

9 Museu Municipal de Loulé

MAP J4 ■ 7 Rua D. Paio Peres Correia ■ Open 9am–6pm Mon–Fri, 9am–2pm Sat ■ Adm (inc castle)

Loulé's archaeological heritage is admirably chronicled with displays of Stone Age, Bronze Age and Roman artifacts. Upstairs, history is closer to the present day, with a reconstruction of a traditional Algarve kitchen, replete with 19th-century crockery and a worn *xarém*, or maize wheel.

10 Museu do Traje, São Brás de Alportel

MAP K4 ■ Rua Dr José Dias Sancho ■ (289) 840 100 ■ Open 10am–1pm & 2–5pm Mon–Fri, 2–5pm Sat & Sun ■ Adm

This delightful ensemble of local costumes, decorated carriages and traditional handicrafts is housed in a wonderful country mansion. A particularly poignant exhibit is a child's faded tunic and breeches next to a wonderful photograph of José Maria Féria wearing the same costume in 1929.

Gramophone, Museu do Traje

🔟 Beaches

1 Praia do Amado, Carrapateira

Pummelled by Atlantic swells, Amado is one of Portugal's premier surfing venues, and its surf school enjoys international patronage. Sitting well off the beaten track, this west coast beach (see p102) also attracts families, and the rock pools at low tide teem with inquisitive children.

2 Praia dos Pescadores, Albufeira

This hugely popular tract of sand (see p85) is characterized by the colourful fishing boats stationed at one end – indeed, its name translates as "Fishermen's Beach". Right in front of the town's old quarter, the beach is reached through a tunnel next to the tourist information office.

3 Praia do Camilo, Lagos

Blessed with gorgeous golden sand lapped by crystal clear waters, Camilo's splendour is enhanced by its scenic location. Flanking the beach (see p102) are rocky cliffs of a rich ochre hue. Outcrops of mustard-red sandstone lie anchored in the shallows. A nearby warren of secluded coves and hidden grottoes can be explored by boat.

Beautiful Praia do Camilo

Secluded Praia de Odeceixe

4 Praia de Odeceixe

One of the Algarve's best-kept secrets, Odeceixe is in a spectacular setting, up in the northwestern corner of the Algarve. Its sheltered, crescent-shaped beach (see p102) is just a short drive (along a road that shadows the path of the river) from the quaint village of Odeceixe. Even in summer, the beach is always wonderfully uncrowded.

5 Praia da Salema, Salema

This select swathe of sand, which lies in front of the fishing village of Salema, is popular with families. The beach also acts as a departure point for some excellent nearby dive sites, such as Boco do Rio to the east, where the wreck of the *Ocean*, an 18th-century French man-of-war, lies in shallow water, now teeming with fish. Make sure you arrive early to find a parking space.

6 Praia de São Rafael, Albufeira

With its shallow waters and soft white sand, Praia da São Rafael *(see p85)* can fill up quickly. Its pretty bay is framed by some extraordinary rock formations, pitted with a number of caves just waiting to be investigated. It offers ideal snorkelling territory and is popular with families.

7 Praia da Ilha de Cabanas

Reached by ferry, and a favourite with kitesurfers *(see p56)*, the secluded sands on Cabanas beach *(see p94)* stretch for more than 7 km (4 miles).

8 Praia da Ilha de Tavira, Tavira
MAP M5

Ostensibly an elongated sandbar, Ilha de Tavira's windward side is a magnet for enthusiasts of water-sports. Opposite Tavira, the wide, sheltered, sandy beach *(see p94)* skirts a campsite and a string of cafés and fine seafood restaurants. There are two access points to this stretch. From Pedras del Rei, you can walk across a causeway or catch a ride on a miniature rail-way. Alternatively, regular ferry boats depart from the jetty at Quatro Águas.

9 Meia Praia, Lagos
MAP D5

A giant curve of sand, 4 km (2 miles) in length makes this the longest beach *(see p102)* in the Algarve. There is plenty of room for water-skiing, windsurfing and jet-skiing, and for sunbathers seeking a little peace and quiet. It also offers a lovely coastal walk, especially in autumn, when the summer tourists have begun to disperse.

The golden sands of Praia da Rocha

10 Praia da Rocha, Portimão

One of the most famous and impressive beaches in the Algarve, Praia da Rocha *(see p85)* is one vast blanket of golden sand set against a backdrop of cinnamon-coloured cliffs. It can become crowded in summer, but a tunnel at the western end allows access to narrower and often quieter stretches of sand. At various points along Avenida Tómas Cabreira, there is further access via steps – some of which are rather steep.

🔟 Coastal Villages and Resort Towns

1 Santa Luzia

An old seafaring myth claims Santa Luzia *(see p92)* came by its foreign-sounding name after an effigy of the Virgin Mary was salvaged from an Italian vessel. Today the image most associated with Santa Luzia is *covos* – octopus pots. This is the octopus capital of the Algarve, and hundreds of the earthenware pots can be found piled neatly on the beach in readiness for their next outing.

2 Alvor
MAP D4

Nestling in a sheltered bay midway between Portimão and Lagos, Alvor is an unusual mix of dignified charm and flickering neon. The old quarter is a delight to wander through, the 16th-century Manueline church is stunning and the village restaurants serve some of the tastiest seafood in the region.

Seafood restaurants in Alvor

The glamorous marina in Vilamoura

3 Vilamoura

Designed around a marina of international repute, this upmarket resort has championship golf courses, a stylish casino, luxury hotels and luxurious villas. Fabulous cruises and boat trips to sea caves depart from the marina *(see p83)*.

4 Salema
MAP C5

Even if you are not staying in Salema, it is worth detouring to it from the EN125 via the beautiful ravine, speckled most of the year with colourful flora and fleet-footed goats. The tarmac peters out where the cobbled slip road begins – a causeway cluttered with colourful fishing boats, rickety lobster pots and shrouds of netting. The sloping streets are banked with salt-laced terraced houses and cramped little tavernas.

The picturesque riverfront at Ferragudo

5 Ferragudo

A maze of cottages, converted lofts and cube-like townhouses tumble down towards the river and Praia Grande – a vast swathe of sand popular with sunbathers and windsurfers. The seafood restaurants lining the tidy quayside of this fishing village *(see p83)* are some of the best in the Algarve.

6 Benagil
MAP F5

Benagil straddles a steep, narrow valley, which ambles its way towards a bay the size of a postage stamp. More hamlet than village, Benagil is blessed with a couple of superb seafood restaurants that are positioned on the lip of the valley and offer great views across the ocean.

7 Monte Gordo
MAP P4

A generous sandy beach and a casino (popular with big spenders from Seville) are the twin targets for most visitors here. Monte Gordo is the closest Algarve beach resort to the Spanish border. The esplanade is fringed with lofty palms, and even loftier apartment blocks, with fabulous views of the ocean.

8 Odeceixe

The isolated splendour of this attractive hillside village *(see pp100–101)* makes the long drive north along the Algarve's western coast worthwhile. An old windmill stands at the village's highest point, and is open to visitors in summer. Odeceixe's beach *(see p48)* is sheltered and peaceful, and it is one of the region's most beautiful.

9 Armação de Pêra
MAP F5

The beach here is one of the longest in the Algarve and fronts a commercial hub of tall apartment blocks, seafront hotels and rows of cafés and bars. However this is all rather clinical, so most visitors head east to Pêra's livelier old town which is spread around the site of a small fortress.

The charming town of Carvoeiro

10 Carvoeiro
MAP E5

Friendliness fills this alluring little town, making it ideal for families. It is one of the Algarve's main self-catering areas, and the hilltops that flank the pocket-sized beach are awash with apartments. On the other side of the promontory is the snorkelling territory of Algar Seco rock formation.

Following pages Praia da Rocha, Portimão

🔟 Inland Villages

1 Salir

The walls of Salir's Moorish castle (see p44) are lit up at night and emit an eerie glow, but on the other side of the village (see p82) the view is considerably more benign, with vistas stretching across the valley from the parish church and garden. In summer this rural idyll is blanketed by narcissi, and alive with the warbling of brightly col-oured passerines.

2 Caldas de Monchique

The warm spa water here has attracted visitors since at least the age of the Roman Empire (see pp20–21). It is just as alluring today, but there are other reasons to visit this hillside hamlet, not least the wood of pine and eucalyptus which provides a lush, cooling canopy in the heat of summer. Woodsmoke and birdsong drift lazily through a valley peppered with whitewashed cottages and smallholdings.

3 Barão de São João
MAP C4

Wrapped in classic hill-walking country and pleasantly lost in time, Barão de São João typifies rural Algarve. It is perhaps best appreciated during the antiques fair, which the village hosts on the last Sunday of every month.

The church in Querença

4 Querença

Surrounded by the rugged Caldeirão mountains, Querença (see p84) is relatively isolated, which is part of its allure. It is best known for its 16th-century church and the ancient, weather-worn cross that stands at the southern edge of the village's picturesque square.

5 Estói

Just off the town's (see p93) main square is the Palácio do Visconde de Estói, a restored 19th-century Rococo palace (now a beautiful pousada), with gardens fanned by giant palms and cooled by fountains. A 20-minute walk from here brings you to Milreu, the

Palácio do Visconde de Estói

remains of a grand Roman villa. The site is dominated by the apse of a temple that was converted into a Christian basilica in the 5th century. The baths, complete with fish mosaics, are another highlight.

6 Alcoutim

The town's *(see p91)* 14th-century castle keeps one timeworn eye on its townsfolk and the other on the old adversary, Sanlúcar, Alcoutim's mirror image on the Spanish side of the River Guadiana. Served by a small ferry, the two villages in different countries are also connected by the only cross-border zip line in the world (www.limitezero.com).

7 Paderne

Early in the 17th century the entire population of Paderne *(see p84)* moved from the shadows of the nearby castle to the environs of a newly consecrated church. That village is now a sleepy place of faded charm and modest means, but therein lies its beauty. The architecture retains a certain grandeur, while the Moorish castle stands close by, perhaps still wondering where all the people went.

8 Guerreiros do Rio
MAP P2

The scenic road south from Alcoutim runs partly along the banks of the River Guadiana and passes through a landscape bristling with olive, fig and carob trees before reaching this tiny village. Amid the orange trees, a former schoolhouse now contains a modest museum that provides a glimpse into the history of the river.

9 Martim Longo
MAP L1 ■ Workshop: 9am– noon Mon–Fri except public hols

The storks nesting on top of the belfry of Martim Longo's parish church have been members of this small community for years, and they are as appealing as their unusual home. The "A Flor da Agulha" dolls' workshop is also worth a visit for its traditional, hand-crafted jute dolls.

A cobbled street in Alte

10 Alte

The village's cobbled streets, colourful window frames and cheerful chimney pots invoke an unhurried air that is quite disarming. Alte's *(see p82)* charming church, situated near a leafy square, retains a fine entrance. The spring running along its flank tumbles under an old mill, providing a great picnic spot.

🔟 Outdoor Pursuits

Kayaking around the unusual rock formations at Praia da Piedade, Lagos

1 Diving
MAP E5 ■ Ocean Revival Park: www.oceanrevival.org

Some wonderful dive sites are found on the Algarve's southwestern coast. The Ocean Revival Park *(see p39)* is an artificial reef composed of four decommissioned navy warships.

2 Cycling and Mountain Biking
MAP K3 ■ Lisa Bikes: www.lisabikes.com

A great way to explore the Algarve is by renting a bicycle. Lisa Bikes arranges self-guided or guided tours, and several mountain-bike adventure companies run cross-country rides.

Cycling near Faro

3 Kayaking
MAP D5 ■ Extreme Algarve: Lagos; www.extremealgarve.com

The Alvor and Ria Formosa estuaries are perfect for kayaking. Discover the sea caves at Ponta da Piedade *(see p26)* with Extreme Algarve.

4 Birdwatching
MAP B5 ■ SPEA: www.spea.pt

Numerous birds are attracted to the Sagres peninsula, Serra de Monchique and Ria Formosa Estuary. The Society for the Study of Birds (SPEA) website has a page devoted to birding tourism (www.birdlife.org).

5 Kite Surfing
MAP N4 ■ Kite Surf Eolis: www.kitesurfeolis.com

Wind conditions off the beaches near Tavira *(see p94)* are particularly good for beginners in kitesurfing. The lagoons around Alvor *(see p50)* are best suited to the more experienced.

6 Big Game Fishing
MAP D5 ■ Blue Shark: Lagos Marina; (916) 788 552; www.blueshark.pt

The Algarve has a long history of fishing, and the warm coastal waters still attract marlin and sharks between June and September. Some operators such as Blue Shark practise a tag and release policy.

7 Ancient Archaeology Tour
MAP B5 ■ Menhir circuit, Hortas do Tabual, Vila do Bispo

Follow a signposted circuit around 5,000-year-old menhirs near the village of Vila do Bispo (see p101).

8 Zip Wire
MAP P1 ■ Limitezero: Sanlúcar de Guadiana; www.limitezero.com

The world's first cross-border zip line ride is a 720-metre cable rigged between the villages of Alcoutim (see p91) and Sanlúcar in Spain.

Surfing the Atlantic waves

9 Surfing
MAP C3 ■ Algarve Surf School: www.algarvesurfschool.com

Algarve's Atlantic rollers provide the perfect conditions for surfing and bodyboarding. Algarve Surf School is one of many excellent camps.

10 Horse Riding
MAP J5 ■ Pinetrees Riding Centre: Corgo da Zorra; (289) 394 369; www.pinetrees.pt

Northwest of Lagos and around Silves is idyllic horse riding territory. Pinetrees Centre offers riding in the Parque Natural da Ria Formosa.

Horse riding in the Algarve

TOP TEN WALKS IN THE ALGARVE

Walking along the Rota Vicentina

1 Rota Vicentina
Connecting Santiago do Cacém with Sagres, this has spectacular coastal scenery (www.rotavicentina.com).

2 Via Algarviana
This trail runs from Alcoutim, in the east, across the region to the Sagres peninsula (www.viaalgarviana.org).

3 Ameixial Circuits
Nature trails set in the Serra da Caldeirão near Ameixial – the location for an annual walking festival.

4 São Lourenço Trail
Set alongside a golf course next to the lagoons and reed beds of the Parque Natural da Ria Formosa.

5 Venta Moinhos Salt Marsh Trail
A route that showcases the Reserva Natural do Sapal (see p91), located near Castro Marim.

6 Benagil–Senhora da Rocha Trail
An occasionally steep clifftop footpath overlooks pretty half-moon coves packed with golden sand.

7 Rocha da Pena Trail
Starting from Penina village, the hike traverses a plateau celebrated for its diversity of flora and fauna.

8 Paderne Castle Trail
Admire the ruins of a Moorish castle (see p44) on this pretty riverside walk.

9 Parque Natural da Ria Formosa Circuit
The trail from the park's HQ passes an old tide mill, Roman salting tanks and observation hides (see pp30–33).

10 Serra de Monchique Mountain Hike
A challenging and rewarding hill walk, with great views, commencing in Monchique (see pp20–21).

Ⓣ🔟 Coastal and River Cruises

① Santa Bernarda Pirate Ship

MAP E4 ■ Rua Júdice Fialho 11, Portimão ■ (967) 023 840 ■ Open Feb–Nov: Mon–Sat ■ www.santa-bernarda.com

Discover caves and coves, before enjoying a beach barbecue, on the exciting themed cruises and special expeditions aboard this pirate ship.

The Santa Bernarda Pirate Ship

② Rio Sul Guadiana

MAP P4 ■ Rua Tristão Vaz Teixeira 15, Monte Gordo ■ (281) 510 200 ■ Open every Tue, Thu (& Sun May–Oct) ■ www.riosultravel.com

A trip along the Guadiana, passing the Reserva Natural do Sapal. Have lunch at Foz de Odeleite and enjoy music and wine on your return.

③ Bom Dia

MAP D5 ■ Marina de Lagos 10 ■ (282) 087 587 ■ Open mid-Mar–Nov ■ www.bomdia-boattrips.com

The colourful Bom Dia schooner sets sail from Lagos harbour for the Ponte de Piedade grottoes, where dinghies allow closer inspection of these natural wonders.

④ Ilha Deserta Cruise

MAP K6 ■ Porta Nova Wharf, Faro ■ (918) 779 155 ■ www.animaris.pt

A maritime expedition through the waterways of the Parque Natural da Ria Formosa is possibly the best way in which to explore this diverse wetland. Lunch is at O Estaminé, which specializes in seafood.

⑤ Dream Wave

MAP G5 ■ Lote 5, Loja 21, Marina de Albufeira ■ (962) 003 885/ 801 ■ www.dreamwavealgarve.com

Enjoy a leisurely cruise on the Leãozinho sailboat, or experience an adrenaline rush on the powerful and rapid Jet Boat or Ocean Rocket.

⑥ Condor de Vilamoura

MAP H5 ■ Cais I 25, Marina de Vilamoura ■ (289) 314 070 ■ Open mid-Mar–Oct ■ www.condordevilamoura.com

Choose between a trip to Albufeira's coastal grottoes or a cruise with a beach barbecue at Armação de Pêra.

The Bom Dia, moored at Lagos Harbour

Boat trip on the Rio Arade

(7) Rio Arade

MAP E4 ■ Esplanade, Portimão ■ (914) 983 967 ■ www.benagil seacave.com

This ancient waterway provides an absorbing journey to Silves (see pp18–19), where you can explore for an hour before returning.

(8) Seafaris

MAP D5 ■ Seafari Stand, Marina de Lagos ■ (282) 798 727 ■ Hours vary seasonally ■ www. seafaris.net

Claiming sightings on 80 per cent of its journeys, this semi-inflatable powers out of the marina. When dolphins are seen, it reduces speed and waits for a display of their antics.

Seagulls on the Ria Formosa

(9) Ria Formosa

MAP K6 ■ Marina de Faro ■ (918) 720 002 ■ www.formosa mar.com

Traditional fishing boats take you through the channels and lagoons of the Parque Natural (see pp30–33).

(10) San Lorenzo Champagne Cruises

MAP H5 ■ Marina de Vilamoura ■ (965) 656 675 ■ www.boatcharter algarve.com

Enjoy a flute of champagne as you step aboard this luxury motor yacht and cruise around in style.

TOP TEN ALGARVE COASTAL AND WETLAND BIRD SPECIES

1 Greater Flamingo
A common resident of the Castro Marim and Ria Formosa areas, especially during the winter.

2 Collared Pratincole
A summer migrant, this wading bird appears in coastal wetlands, particularly the Castro Marim marshes.

3 Audouin's Gull
A large gull distinguished by its stubby red bill. Although present all year, its numbers swell in winter.

4 Spoonbill
A long-legged wading bird seen in coastal lagoons all year, but especially abundant in winter.

5 Caspian Tern
The Alvor estuary and Castro Marim marshes are favourite winter habitats for the world's largest tern.

6 Kentish Plover
A ubiquitous shorebird present all year, it is very easy to observe along the Ria Formosa and Alvor estuaries.

7 Black-winged Kite
Winter is the best time to spot this sleek raptor. Habitats include the Vilamoura reed beds.

8 Red-rumped Swallow
The Arade and Guadiana riverbanks are the preferred nesting sites for this handsome summer species.

9 Glossy Ibis
Its shiny reddish-brown body and bottle-green wings lend this winter wader its name.

10 Black-winged Stilt
Arguably the most symbolic of resident Algarvean waders; its habitats include the wetlands near Faro.

A black-winged stilt in wetlands

🔟 Golf Courses

Penina Academy golf course

① Penina Academy Course
MAP E4 ■ Penina Hotel & Golf Resort, Penina, near Portimão ■ www.penina.com

A compact, 9-hole course laid out amid the Championship fairways, the ease of play here should relax even the most nervous of players. The adjoining golf academy offers individual or group tuition.

② Royal Course, Vale do Lobo
MAP J5 ■ Royal Golf Course, Vale do Lobo ■ www.valedolobo.com

A rolling terrain abundant with pine envelopes this par 72 layout. The highlight is the infamous 16th, where a powerful and accurate swing is needed to carry a set of precipitous cliffs before the green. The signature hole is the 9th, with its spectacular, semi-island green.

③ San Lorenzo
In the Parque Natural da Ria Formosa, and one of the top five golf courses in continental Europe, the par 72 layout culminates with a green on the 18th that must be approached from across a lake. Part of the Dona Filipa & San Lorenzo Golf Resort *(see p127)*, the course *(see p86)* is open to visitors, with priority given to hotel guests. The clubhouse restaurant has a lovely terrace with views over the greens.

④ Pine Cliffs
With a clifftop layout, this 9-hole golf course *(see p86)* is set against an ocean backdrop and offers spectacular views. The course hides under a canopy of umbrella pine, with narrow fairways demanding a steady swing. The final hole requires a shot from the "Devil's Parlour" clifftop tee that will carry a deep ravine to hit the green.

⑤ Victoria
MAP H5 ■ Anantara Vilamoura Algarve Resort ■ www.anantara.com/en/vilamoura-algarve

Designed by golf legend Arnold Palmer, this undulating 18-hole par 72 layout is regarded as one of the best and most sophisticated courses in Europe. It features wide fairways and extensive water hazards.

Royal Course, Vale do Lobo

6 Gramacho Course, Pestana Carvoeiro

MAP E5 ■ Pestana Golf & Resort, Carvoeiro ■ www.pestanagolf.com

Gramacho gained another 9-hole layout to add to the original double 9, and the combination allows for a variety of options in pin settings and length to suit those with a high or a low handicap.

7 Balaia

Popular with beginners, as well as with the more adroit, this layout (see p86) is recommended for the holiday golfer who prefers a fairly relaxed game. It still requires a degree of concentration, however, especially when it comes to club selection, as the holes vary in length more than one might expect in a 9-hole course.

8 Quinta do Lago South

This par 72 championship course (see p86) within the estate of the same name has hosted the Portuguese Open on several occasions, and is one of the flagship European Tour courses. The undulating layout favours long hitters, but strategic bunkering, the odd water hazard and large, contoured greens provide plenty of challenges. Despite its championship status, the course welcomes golfers of all abilities, and has two well-equipped clubhouses.

9 Quinta da Ria

MAP N4 ■ Quinta da Ria, near Vila Nova de Cacela ■ www.quintadaria.com

Bordering the Parque Natural da Ria Formosa (see pp30–33), this 18-hole par 72 layout golf course is said to be one of the best in the region and offers great ocean views. The five lakes were built to provide natural obstacles in the course of the game and also to support the flora and fauna. The many carob, olive and almond trees are now home to numerous species.

The 18-hole Quinta da Ria golf course

10 Monte Rei

MAP N4 ■ Monte Rei Golf & Country Club, Sesmarias ■ www.monte-rei.com

The celebrated Jack Nicklaus designed this par 72 championship course, part of an upmarket country club located behind Vila Nova de Cacela. The layout is known for its ingeniously shaped bunkers and challenging water hazards. Facilities include a plush clubhouse and a highly regarded golf academy.

ᴛᴏᴘ10 Children's Attractions

The Almancil Karting circuit

1 Almancil Karting

MAP J5 ■ Vale d'Éguas, Almancil ■ Open 2–7pm Tue, 10am–7pm Wed–Sun (hours may vary according to seasons) ■ Adm ■ www.kartingalgarve.com

Experience life in the fast lane at this challenging circuit, catering for everyone. Two-seater karts (for an adult and child to ride together) and karts adapted for people with reduced mobility are available.

2 Parque da Mina

MAP E3 ■ Sítio do Vale de Boi, Caldas de Monchique ■ (962) 079 408 ■ Open Oct–Mar: 10am–5pm; Apr–Sep: 10am–7pm; closed Nov–Mar: Mon & Tue ■ Adm

An adventure theme park, complete with a playground and heritage centre. With advanced booking, the energetic may traverse a lofty rope slide. Visitors can try and find their way out of a mirror maze, the park's latest attraction.

3 Krazy World Zoo

MAP G4 ■ Lagoa de Viseu, near Algoz ■ Open 10am–6pm daily (Jul & Aug: to 6:30pm; winter hours vary) ■ Adm ■ www.krazyworld.com

Snakes and alligators are among the residents at this highly entertaining animal park. The pet farm is sanctuary to smaller, more cuddly creatures. Children can enjoy pony rides, play a round of mini-golf or have fun in the inflatable playground.

4 Zoomarine

MAP G5 ■ Estrada Nacional 125, Guia ■ Open mid-Mar–Oct: 10am–6pm daily (Jul & Aug: to 7:30pm) ■ Adm ■ www.zoomarine.pt

Promoting conservation and environmental education, Zoomarine has seal, dolphin and sea lion presentations, tropical birds and bird-of-prey shows. A water slide, funfair and 4D cinema are among the many other attractions.

A sea lion at Zoomarine

Previous pages Staircase decorated with tiles, Pousada Palácio de Estói

Children enjoying some of the attractions at Slide & Splash

5 Slide & Splash
MAP E4 ▪ Estrada 125, Vale de Deus, Estômbar, near Lagoa ▪ Open Apr–Oct: 10am–5:30pm daily (summer: to 6pm); closed Apr & Oct: Sun ▪ Adm ▪ www.slidesplash.com

Corkscrew, Disco River and the Big Wave are some of the best water chutes at this fun waterpark. The adrenaline rush starts working overtime when you are halfway down the Banzai water slide.

6 Aquashow Family Park
MAP H5 ▪ Semino, near Quarteira ▪ Open May–Sep: daily ▪ Adm ▪ www.aquashowpark.com

The Free Fall water slide at this theme park is the only one of its kind in Europe and is a ride to remember. Other favourites are the White Fall, Water Coaster and Wild Snake water chutes, which the biggest in Europe. Toddlers can paddle in Aqualand – the playground is in the swimming pool.

7 Lagos Adventure Park
MAP D5 ▪ Albardeira, Meia Praia, Lagos ▪ Opening times vary (depends on weather) ▪ Adm ▪ www.lusoaventura.com

With high rope courses of varying difficulty levels, set in the trees of a pine forest near the beach, this park offers adventure and entertainment for all. Participants move through a series of obstacles as they make their way through "cobwebs", climb vertical nets and traverse numerous rope ladders. Other exciting activities, such as paintball, are also on offer.

8 Family Golf Park
MAP H5 ▪ Rua dos Marmeleiros, Vilamoura ▪ (289) 300 800 ▪ Open Feb–Nov: from 10am daily (closing times vary) ▪ Adm ▪ www.familygolfpark.pt

A great attraction for the whole family, where two 18-hole mini-golf courses test the skills of both children and parents. Catch the tourist train that tours Vilamoura before returning for refreshments at the café.

9 FIESA International Sand Sculpture Festival
MAP F4 ▪ Between Pêra and Algoz ▪ Open Mar, Sep & Nov: 10am–7pm daily; Jun & Jul: 10am–10pm daily ▪ Closing times vary ▪ Adm ▪ www.fiesa.org

The Algarve's international sand sculpture festival brings together some of the world's most talented artists. The huge sculptures are illuminated at night.

10 Lagos Zoological Park
MAP D4 ▪ Estrada Municipal de Bensafrim, Barão de S. João ▪ Open 10am–5pm daily (summer: to 7pm) ▪ Adm ▪ www.zoolagos.com

Lemurs, gibbons and Vietnamese pigs share the grounds with graceful flamingoes, leggy emus, toucans and bouncing walla-bies. The lynxes are a highlight.

Flamingo at Lagos Zoo

🔟 Clubs and Late-Night Bars

① Kiss, Albufeira

One of the most famous of all the Algarve's nightclubs, Kiss (see p88) is known for its memorable party nights and quirky theme festivals. Three dance floors reverberate to a mixture of cutting-edge house, techno and hip-hop, attracting seasoned clubbers from all over the continent. Kiss starts to heat up at around 3am and is still sizzling at dawn.

Trendy bar area at NoSoloÁgua

② NoSoloÁgua, Praia da Rocha

MAP E5 ■ Marina de Portimão–Praia da Rocha ■ Open summer: 10am–3am daily ■ www.nosoloagua.com

Located right on the beach, this chic bar and restaurant is a favourite hangout for a young, fashionable crowd. Live-music nights feature an eclectic range of styles, from blues and bossa nova to traditional jazz and fado. Guest DJs spin tracks on Saturday nights. Sunset parties take place around the swimming pool and continue after dark. Entry is free until 1am.

③ Bar Amuras, Lagos

MAP D5 ■ Marina del Lagos, Lagos ■ Open 10am–2am daily

A popular lunchtime haunt, this bar buzzes at night with a mix of funky DJ sounds and occasional live music. Also a popular sports bar, it broadcasts live events on big screens.

④ Round Up Saloon, Carvoeiro

MAP E5 ■ 1 Estrada do Farol, Praia do Carvoeiro ■ Open 8pm–2am daily; closed Nov–Mar

At this happening bar, the "outlaws" are locked up in a "jail" on the whim of Big Will, the bartender, and are freed only on the promise of a beer. On most nights, there is live rock music and budding musicians are invited to jam. On Tuesday, Thursday and Saturday nights the karaoke cavalry arrives.

⑤ Stevie Ray's Live Music Bar, Lagos

MAP D5 ■ 9 Rua Srº da Graça, Lagos ■ Open 9am–4am Tue–Sat (hours vary in winter)

Live music on Friday and Saturday nights lifts this already excellent late-night bar to new heights. The atmosphere swings from jazz and blues to soul and house.

6 Katedral, Praia da Rocha

Katedral's three bars *(see p88)* flank a central dance floor that is never big enough to accommodate the throngs of party people dancing until the early hours of the morning. The ambience and music make it a favourite with locals and tourists. A sprawling terrace bar at the back offers great views of the beach and is an ideal chill-out spot.

7 Le Club Santa Eulália, Albufeira

A stylish and sophisticated nightclub close to the beach and attached to 5-star hotel Grande Real Santa Eulália *(see p125)*. The club *(see p88)* has four different zones, including an excellent à la carte restaurant that offers a range of dishes complemented with an extensive wine list, and the main dance floor overlooks an ocean-front terrace with spectacular views. This trendy club hosts internationally-renowned DJs. A smart-casual dress code is enforced.

8 Ubi, Tavira

MAP M4 ■ Rua Almirante Candido dos Reis, Tavira ■ Open 11pm–4am daily (Fri & Sat: to 6am); hours vary in winter

Housed in an abandoned warehouse, Ubi is a fashionable disco lounge. It is eastern Algarve's premier late-night hot spot. Head to The Terrace (the dance floor) and party the night away, or chill out and chat with friends at The Factory – the lounge area of this trendy club.

The dance floor at Kadoc

Libertos' stylish esplanade

9 Libertos, Albufeira

MAP G5 ■ Areias de São João, Albufeira ■ Open summer: 8pm–4am daily ■ www.libertosclub.com

One of the region's best nightclubs, Libertos rivals Kiss in popularity. Football and TV stars are often among its summertime clientele. The esplanade (a favourite location for fashion shows) comes complete with a swimming pool and palm trees. Inside, a giant screen relays 24-hour cable TV broadcasts. By midnight, however, the DJ takes centre stage.

10 Kadoc, Vilamoura

A sprawling venue of gigantic proportions, Kadoc nightclub *(see p88)* can accommodate up to 7,000 party-goers on five-tiered dance floors, illuminated by a spectacular tricolour laser system. The clientele is young and energetic. A landscaped open-air terrace set in a tropical garden offers a great spot for those chill-out sessions. It is one of the last clubs to wind down, closing at around 7am.

🔟 Culinary Highlights of the Algarve

1 Sardinhas Assadas

The humble and ubiquitous sardine is arguably the most popular menu choice in the region. Bursting with goodness, sardines are at their plumpest during summer, and are simply mouth-watering when charcoal-grilled and served with boiled potatoes and salad.

Classic *porco à Alentejana*

***Sardinhas assadas,* a popular dish**

2 Amêijoas na Cataplana

If there is one dish synonymous with the Algarve's rich ocean harvest, it's this one. Fresh cockles are sealed in a *cataplana*, a rounded copper cooking vessel resembling a wok. Allowed to cook in their own steam with a combination of *presunto* (cured ham), *chouriço* (sausage), tomato, lemon, olive oil and garnished with coriander and garlic, the result is a succulent seafood delight. It is best enjoyed with chilled white wine.

3 Porco à Alentejana

This intrepid marriage of pork and clams appears to bring the ocean and the countryside together, although it's a feast that originated in the vast plains of the Alentejo. The ingredients are cooked in a spicy marinade of white wine, fresh garlic and paprika. If the dish is prepared correctly, the shells should be open when served.

4 Arroz de Polvo

A regional speciality which again evokes the Algarve's love affair with the sea. Tender morsels of fresh octopus are added to a mix of fried onion and parsley, and then gently boiled with wine vinegar and a dash of chilli powder. Rice is added, with salt and pepper to taste. The meal is usually served with a side dish of black olives and generous slices of crusty bread.

5 Doces de Amêndoa

Almonds (another Moorish import) are used to make these colourful little delicacies that can look like fish, fruit, birds, smiling faces and even vegetable baskets.

6 Cabrito Assado

Roasted kid is one of the gastronomical wonders of the rural Algarve. The meat is brushed with a thin layer of lard, sprinkled with minced bacon and laced with white wine. Garnished with whole garlic cloves and dusted with paprika, it is slowly roasted until crispy brown.

Delicious *amêijoas na cataplana*

7 Gaspacho do Algarve

This version of gazpacho soup differs from its well-known Spanish counterpart in that the ingredients are not pulverized, enabling it to retain a delightfully crunchy texture. Served cold, this heavenly blend of tomato, garlic, cucumber, oregano and sweet pepper sprinkled with diced crouton is bliss on a hot day.

8 Bifes de Atum

The livelihoods of whole communities used to depend on tuna. It is not fished so hard now, but is still a favourite in thousands of restaurants along the coast. Try *atum de cebola*, a tasty blend of melted butter and tomato sauce with onions, garlic and parsley, poured over a firm tuna steak garnished with lemon wedges.

9 Morgado de Figo

Figs were introduced by the Moors and soon became an integral part of Algarvian cuisine. Fig lord cakes are dainty creations moulded from a fig-and-almond paste.

Frango assado com piri-piri

10 Frango Assado com Piri-Piri

The great Portuguese standby: some restaurants in the Algarve serve nothing else. Generous platters of juicy chicken portions are served with crisp French fries and green-pepper salad. The meat comes with optional red chilli sauce, which is homemade and usually hot.

TOP 10 ALGARVE WINES, LIQUEURS AND SPIRITS

Bottles of Medronho

1 Medronho
The celebrated *aguardente* (brandy) is produced commercially, but the best is the "Monchique Moonshine", which is distilled in secret and sold with a nod and a wink.

2 Tapada da Torre
The flagship label *(see p87)* from local winemaker João O'Neill Mendes. Both red and white are exceptionally smooth on the palate.

3 Quê
A sparkling rosé made at the Barranco Longo vineyard from the *touriga nacional* grape.

4 Vida Nova
Wine produced from Sir Cliff Richard's Algarve estate *(see p72)*. With a rich, spicy bouquet, this red sings of young berry fruit.

5 Amarguinha
A sweet bitter-almond liqueur from the Algarve. It is ideal as an apéritif or as a digestif.

6 Barranco Longo
The Reserva Red is produced from *touriga nacional* and *syrah* grapes.

7 Aperitivo Algarseco
An underrated Algarvian dry white apéritif wine, which is similar to an amontillado.

8 Licor de Tangerina
Wonderfully fragrant liqueur with the tang of lush citrus groves.

9 Brandy-mel
A potent mix of brandy and honey, this is a favourite mid-winter tipple.

10 Odelouca River Valley
Expressive, elegant and very well-balanced red wine from the Quinta do Francês winery *(see p72)*.

🔟 Restaurants

Atmospheric terrace at Casa Velha

① Casa Velha, Quinta do Lago

French haute cuisine is served in this 300-year-old converted farmhouse *(see p89)*, with an attractive outdoor terrace. With more than 200 Portuguese red wines to choose from, it will appeal to wine connoisseurs and seasoned gourmets alike. Dishes served include the Marbré of Duck Foie Gras with figs and the King Crab with Ossetra Caviar.

② Brisa do Rio, Tavira

This friendly backstreet eatery *(see p95)* has received glowing praise for its outstanding regional fare, such as black pork *cataplana* (casserole) with clams. An outdoor seating area is also available.

③ O Barradas, Silves

Set in a converted country farmhouse, this restaurant *(see p89)* has a comfortable indoor seating area, complete with a fireplace. It also offers guests the option to dine outside in the garden, or on the covered terrace. The dishes served here are modern takes on traditonal Portuguese cuisine. Culinary highlights include baked wild fish and the *Mirandesa* (veal served with fig chutney).

④ Adega Vila Lisa, Mexilhoeira Grande

Renowned Portuguese food critic José Quitério regards this charming rural eatery *(see p105)* as one of the best in the country. The five-course tasting menu features traditional dishes such as *canja de conquilhas* (cockle broth), but it changes daily, depending on what's fresh and available. Make sure you book well in advance as the restaurant is very popular, particularly in peak season.

⑤ O Terraço, Martinhal

Traditional Portuguese cuisine is offered with flair and imagination at this contemporary restaurant *(see p105)*. Serving hotel and resort guests, as well as non-residents, the emphasis is family-oriented, and the menu will appeal to both refined tastes and young palates.

⑥ Mirandus, Lagos

This enchanting gourmet restaurant *(see p105)* is perched on the top of a cliff with stunning views out to sea. You can choose from a five-course set menu, which changes every day, or make your selections à la carte. The menu is put together by the resident chef, and specially

Stunning views from the Mirandus

focuses on fresh seasonal and local produce. Vegetarian and vegan options are available alongside authentic meat and fish dishes. The wine list is an inspiration in itself. Be sure to book in advance.

Waterfront views at Sueste

7 Sueste, Ferragudo
The bizarre-looking but incredibly tasty *imperador* (emperor fish) is one of the more unusual treats on offer at this fabulous quayside restaurant *(see p89)* overlooking the River Arade. Spectacular summer sunsets bathe the terrace with a golden light, adding greatly to Sueste's appeal. Seafood dominates the menu, and you can watch the chef grilling the catch of the day by the waterfront.

8 Ocean, Alporchinhos
MAP F5 ■ Vila Vita Parc, Rua Anneliese Pohl, Alporchinhos ■ (282) 310 100 ■ Closed Tue ■ Reservations required ■ No veg dishes ■ www.restauranteocean.com ■ €€€
Dishes such as red mullet, Spello beans and Andalusian prawn have

earned chef Hans Neuner and his team two Michelin stars. The international wine list is excellent.

9 Veneza, Paderne
A warm atmosphere pervades this exceptional family-run restaurant *(see p89)*. The traditional cuisine is straight out of grandma's kitchen – hearty country fare prepared from hand-me-down recipes. The award-winning wine cellar heaves with more than 1,000 labels which are all stored under excellent conditions.

10 Vila Joya, Albufeira
An exclusive gourmet restaurant, the Villa Joya *(see p89)* has two Michelin stars to its name. Austrian chef Dieter Koschina's inventive take on traditional Portuguese cuisine uses northern European techniques. Experienced sommeliers help in pairing the excellent dishes with the best wines.

Pretty poolside setting at Vila Joya

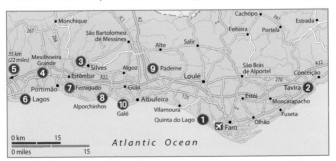

For a key to restaurant price ranges see p89

⭘ Wineries

① Quinta do Francês
MAP E4 ▪ Sítio da Dobra, Odelouca ▪ (282) 106 303 ▪ Open mid-Mar–mid-Nov: 10am–1pm & 2–5:30pm Tue–Sun; mid-Nov–mid-Mar: 10am–1pm & 2–5:30pm Mon–Fri ▪ Advance booking for groups ▪ www.quintadofrances.com

Wines from here (see p19) are found in some of the Algarve's finest restaurants, and have an international reputation. Tastings are hosted in the wine shop where you can buy the flagship, Quinta do Francês Syrah red.

Quinta do Francês wine shop

② Quinta do Barradas
MAP F4 ▪ Sítio da Venda Nova, near Silves ▪ (282) 443 308 ▪ Open 3–6pm Thu–Tue ▪ Advance booking required ▪ www.obarradas.com

Cultivated by the same team that runs O Barradas restaurant (see p89), the vineyard is a complementary venture that has resulted in some fruity and exuberant wines, notably the Quinta do Barradas Selecção. Tours take in the winery and a boutique wine store. The wines produced on the property are, of course, stocked in the restaurant's cellar.

③ Quinta dos Vales
MAP E4 ▪ Sítio dos Vales, near Estombar ▪ (282) 431 036 ▪ Open 9am–1pm & 2–6pm Mon–Fri (summer: to 7pm daily) ▪ Guided wine tasting and tour: advanced booking required ▪ www.quintadosvales.eu

One of the region's leading producers, this verdant estate is renowned for its many award-winning wines, among them the celebrated Marquês dos Vales Grace Touriga-Nacional. Besides the winery, tours take in extensive gardens where colourful and quirky sculpture is exhibited. Visitors can also take part in art workshops. On-site accommodation is available for those wishing to linger.

④ Quinta da Vinha
MAP F4 ▪ Sítio da Vala, near Lagoa ▪ (912) 104 557 ▪ Open 9am–6pm Mon–Fri ▪ Advance booking required ▪ www.josemanuelcabrita. wix.com/quintadavinha

Despite basic amenities, this winery is worth investigating for its delightfully understated appeal that belies the quality of the wines produced. Visitors can taste three different wines – red, white and rosé – served with a delicious selection of hams, cheeses and smoked sausage. The Cabrita Reserva 2014, an "intense and heavenly" red, is a must-have bottle to take away.

⑤ Adega do Cantor
MAP G4 ▪ Quinta do Miradouro, Guia ▪ (968) 776 971 ▪ Open 10am–1pm & 2–5pm daily ▪ Guided tours: advance booking required ▪ www. winesvidanova.com

Sir Cliff Richard is the celebrity name behind the "Winery of the Singer" – the vineyard is on his property near Albufeira. After a tour visitors can taste wines from the Vida Nova and Onda Nova range. An open-air terrace overlooks one of the vineyards.

Lovely views at Adega do Cantor

6 Quinta Rosa

MAP F4 ■ Pinheiro e Garrado, near Silves ■ (968) 986 393 ■ Closed Aug ■ Guided tours only: advance booking required ■ www.quinta-rosa.nl

This relatively new, Dutch-run vineyard is behind the select Uit de Kelders Van Jaap wine label. Utilizing organic farming techniques, the estate produced its first harvest in 2011 and now offers tours, tastings and plenty of amusing anecdotes. Volunteers can help with grape picking in exchange for board and lodging.

7 Quinta João Clara

MAP F4 ■ Vale de Lousas, near Alcantarilha ■ (967) 012 444 ■ Open 9am–6pm daily ■ Advance booking required ■ www.joaoclara.com

No fewer than six wines are produced at this family-run vineyard, which occupies land farmed since the 1970s. Well respected in industry circles (the João Clara red is a multi-award winner), the various wines can be tasted as part of a tour of the premises. For added flavour, visitors can request an optional ham and cheese accompaniment.

8 Quinta da Penina

MAP E4 ■ Rua da Angola Lote 2, Loja B+C, Portimão ■ (282) 491 070 ■ Guided tours only: advance booking required ■ www.vinhosportimao.com

Tours of the estate near Alvor (see p50) are conducted for groups of ten or more. Tastings allow a variety of wines to be sampled, representing two separate labels. Mid-range choices include the Foral de Portimão Petit-Verdot red and, for a treat, the elegant and full-flavoured Quinta da Penina Reserva.

9 Monte da Casteleja

MAP D4 ■ Sargaçal, near Lagos ■ (282) 798 408 ■ Open 3–5pm Tue–Thu; Shop: 9am–1pm daily ■ Advance booking required ■ www.montecasteleja.com

The grapes used to produce the highly regarded reds, whites and rosés at this tranquil winery are grown organically here (see p27). Rustic-style accommodation is also available.

Rustic Monte da Casteleja

10 Quinta do Morgado da Torre

MAP D4 ■ Sítio da Penina, Torre ■ (282) 476 866 ■ Visits 10am–noon & 2–5pm Mon–Fri ■ Advance booking for groups ■ www.morgadodatorre.com

Integrated within a working farm located near the coast, wines produced here (see p38) benefit from the mild influence of sea breezes. As a result, expect well-structured wines with generous fruity aromas. There is a tour of the winery which concludes in the farm shop for tastings.

Shopping Malls and Markets

1 Quinta Shopping, Quinta do Lago

This elegant mall *(see p87)* with its open-air terraces and wide esplanades is situated within the exclusive Quinta do Lago estate. Well-known fashion houses showcase their latest ready-to-wear designs, and there are some top-range jewellery, cosmetics and perfumes for sale. This is the place to go if you are looking to spend some serious cash.

Elegant Quinta shopping mall

2 Algarve Shopping, Guia

The exterior of this shopping complex *(see p87)* is striking in its colour scheme, following the geometric pattern of traditional Algarve architecture. Inside, the mall boasts more than 130 stores, 45 fashion boutiques, a hypermarket as well as a food hall.

The expansive Forum Algarve

3 Quarteira Fish Market

One of the best-loved fish markets *(see p87)* in the region, where the catch is landed at dawn and on sale by 8:30am. Be prepared to haggle on prices and to compete with others for the best fish. Note that the throng is usually largest around the famous Quarteira prawns.

4 Olhão Market

MAP L5 ■ Avenida 5 de Outubro, Olhão ■ Open 7am–2pm Tue–Fri, 6:30am–3pm Sat

Situated right on the esplanade overlooking the lagoons, this is a fantastic place to shop for fresh fish, fruit and vegetables and flowers. A riot of noise and colour takes place under two purpose-built pavilions. On Saturdays it is enlivened by extra stalls selling anything from basketware and smoked sausage, to honey and lace.

5 Forum Algarve, Faro

Forum Algarve is the biggest mall *(see p87)* of its kind in the whole region, attracting visitors and residents alike. More than 100 shops, boutiques and department stores, as well as an enormous hypermarket, multi-screen cinema and family entertainment centre, are imaginatively incorporated into an architectural design inspired by Faro's historic city centre.

6 Aqua Portimão
MAP E4 ∎ Rua de São Pedro 72, Portimão ∎ Open 9am–11pm daily (to midnight Fri & Sat, Jul, Aug & Dec) ∎ www.aquaportimao.pt

Centrally located, this modern shopping mall features nearly 80 shops, boutiques and a huge hypermarket. There are several ATMs, and underground car parking is free. The top floor is all restaurants.

7 Apolónia Supermarket, Galé
MAP J5 ∎ Sítio Vale do Rebelho, Galé ∎ Open 8am–8pm daily (summer: to 9pm)

Shoppers in the know travel here from across the length and breadth of the region. The market features foreign produce such as fresh Argentinian beef, macaroni pasta and spicy tandoori curry powder. The cosmopolitan wine selection includes bottles from California, Chile and Australia. There are two other branches, one in Almancil (see p87) and another in Lagoa.

8 Armação de Pêra Fruit and Fish Market
MAP F5 ∎ Behind Largo da Igreja, Armação de Pêra ∎ Open 7am–1pm Wed & Sat

This indoor and outdoor market has an amazing choice of fresh fruit and fish, including crab, lobster and clams. Outside you will find stalls selling jams, honey and tongue-tingling *piri-piri*.

Urn, Porches Pottery

9 Porches Pottery
The blue and white façade of this building (see p87) is unmistakable, and the pottery produced here is equally striking. All the pottery and earthenware on sale has been manufactured in-house, and you can see rows of locals gossiping merrily amongst themselves while deftly applying paint to the latest batch of crockery.

10 Loulé Market
This daily market (see p87) bursts with the freshest harvest from the ocean and the hinterland. Delicate sprigs of herbs and spices hang over pots of honey and jam. Cakes made from fig and almond compete for space with loops of smoked sausage, glistening fresh fish, and the numerous blooms of bright, fragrant flowers.

An array of produce at Loulé Market

🔟 Festivals and Events

Flower Torches Festival

1 Flower Torches Festival
MAP K4 ■ São Brás de Alportel town centre ■ Easter Sun

Dozens of suited men holding aloft elaborate bouquets of flower torches line a "flower pavement" – a series of roads decorated with carpets of colourful petals that a religious procession follows as it makes its way towards the parish church. Set near the church, a handicrafts fair opens mid-morning, and there's another fair selling local delicacies at Largo S. Sebastião.

2 Mãe Soberana, Loulé
MAP J4 ■ Loulé town centre ■ Usually last week in Apr

This is the Algarve's most important religious festival, linked to ancient maternity rites. On the second Sunday after Easter (Festa Grande), a 16th-century statue of Mãe Soberana (the Sovereign Mother) is carried into town from her hilltop shrine. Exuding solemnity and piety, the subdued procession makes its way to Loulé's parish church where the image rests for two weeks. On the return journey the mood is more ebullient – flowers are tossed at the cortège, and there are cries of "Viva Mãe Soberana!"

3 Festival Med, Loulé
MAP J4 ■ Loulé ■ Last week in Jun ■ www.festivalmed.pt

This festival celebrates Mediterranean and North African culture through concerts, culinary events, art exhibitions as well as children's activities, held in and around Loulé. It also includes world-class acts from Brazil, the Caribbean and sub-Saharan Africa. Many of the town's monuments – such as the castle and Islamic bathhouse (see pp22–3) – serve as festival venues.

4 International Motorbike Meeting, Faro
MAP K6 ■ Vale das Almas, Faro ■ Mid-Jul ■ www.motoclubefaro.pt ■ Adm

This festival attracts thousands of bikers and motorbike enthusiasts to the capital of the Algarve for a weekend of music concerts, classic motorbike exhibitions, a trade fair and various other motorbike-related activities. Hosted by Moto Clube Faro, this festival is the largest of its kind in Portugal and is well established on the region's festival calendar.

(5) Portimão Sardine Festival
MAP E4 ■ Portimão riverfront ■ Usually 1st week in Aug

Generally regarded as the sardine capital of the Algarve, Portimão throws a big party in summer to honour this venerable fish. Revellers are drawn to the riverfront by live music and the delicious aroma of grilled sardines. On the last night, there is a huge firework display.

(6) Silves Medieval Fair
MAP F4 ■ Silves ■ Second week in Aug ■ Adm for jousting displays

Silves returns to its former medieval splendour during this festival, when the centre's narrow streets and alleys become one huge souk. Visitors can enjoy parades, live music, street theatre and jousting competitions.

Silves Medieval Fair

(7) Seafood Festival, Olhão
MAP L5 ■ Jardim Patrão Joaquim Lopes, Olhão ■ 10–15 Aug ■ www.festivaldomarisco.com

Olhão is the Algarve's biggest fishing port, and at festival time numerous stalls groan under the weight of every imaginable seafood delicacy, including octopus, squid, clam, prawn, mussel and the ubiquitous grilled sardine. Folk music and dancing add further flavour.

(8) Fatacil, Lagoa
MAP E4 ■ Fatacil showground, EN 125, Lagoa ■ Mid-Aug ■ www.fatacil.pt ■ Adm

The premier showcase for all things Algarve, this nine-day jamboree attracts visitors from all over Portugal. It is part agricultural show, part handicrafts fair – with a music concert, trade exhibition and gastronomy festival thrown in for good measure.

(9) Medieval Fair, Castro Marim
MAP P3 ■ Castro Marim ■ Last week in Aug ■ Adm

For a few days towards the end of the summer the town of Castro Marim returns to the Middle Ages to host a spectacular pageant and fair in the grounds of the 13th-century castle. Archers draw their bows on mock bullseye targets while mounted knights tilt their lances, and jesters entertain the crowd with medieval music and banter. At night, actors in period costume recreate medieval plays before a hushed audience.

(10) Algarve Classic Car Festival
MAP D4 ■ Autódromo Internacional do Algarve, Mexilhoeira Grande ■ 3rd weekend in Oct ■ www.autodromodoalgarve.com ■ Adm

Hundreds of legendary sports cars can be seen at this remarkable annual event. Various races take place for different categories of vehicle. Previous events have attracted many celebrated drivers such as Sir Stirling Moss.

Algarve Classic Car Festival

The Algarve Area by Area

Sea caves at Ponta da Piedade, Lagos

🔟 Central Region

The Algarve's central region encompasses the busiest coastal resorts in southern Portugal as well as remote inland hamlets. It is an area of contrasting character, with beautiful golden beaches and wild, rolling hills where a more traditional, rural way of life prevails. History has left its indelible mark throughout this land in the shape of Stone Age megaliths, the remains of Roman villas, Moorish castles and Gothic cathedrals. A strong, proud maritime heritage pervades the coast, evident in the many fine seafood restaurants.

1 Silves

The capital of the Algarve during Moorish rule, Silves overlooks a fertile valley of lemon and orange groves, cork and almond trees and scented meadows. The town's main draw is its castle: as well as taking an inspiring walk around its battlements, visitors should look out for the vaulted Moorish cistern and traitor's gate – the battle-scarred doorway through which Dom Paio Peres Correia stormed to recapture the stronghold for Christian forces in 1242. Outside the castle walls is the 13th-century cathedral (*see pp18–19*), which was the seat of the Algarve see until 1580.

2 Albufeira

Albufeira's claim as the most popular holiday destination in the country is no idle boast. It is the

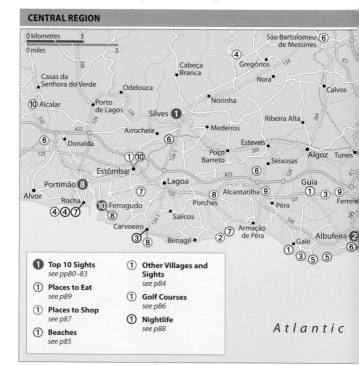

CENTRAL REGION

0 kilometres 5
0 miles 5

São Bartolomeu de Messines ⑥
④ Gregórios
Cabeça Branca
Nora
Calvos
Casas da Senhora do Verde
Odelouca
Norinha
⑩ Alcalar
Porto de Lagos
Silves ❶
Ribeira Alta
Arrochela
Medeiros
⑥ Donalda
⑥
Estevais
Poço Barreto
Algoz Tunes
① ⑩
Seixosas
Estômbar
Lagoa
Guia
① ③ ⑨
Portimão ❽
⑦
⑧ Alcantarilha ⑨
Ferreir
Alvor
Rocha
Porches
Péra
④④⑦ ⑩ Ferragudo
⑧
Salicos
⑧ Carvoeiro
⑦ Armação de Péra
Albufeira ❷
③⑧ Benagil ②
① Galé
③⑤ ⑤

Atlantic

❶ **Top 10 Sights** *see pp80–83*	① **Other Villages and Sights** *see p84*
① **Places to Eat** *see p89*	① **Golf Courses** *see p86*
① **Places to Shop** *see p87*	① **Nightlife** *see p88*
① **Beaches** *see p85*	

Praia do Inatel, a popular beach in Albufeira

biggest and most energetic resort *(see pp36–7)* in the Algarve, and anyone looking for a lively night out should make a midsummer beeline to the area dubbed "The Strip". A forest of neon lends the resort its exotic, all-night atmosphere, and a multitude of bars, restaurants and clubs keep the party swinging until dawn. In the daytime, you can catch up on sleep on any one of Albufeira's smooth, golden beaches.

3 Faro

Faro is often overlooked by visitors to the Algarve who tend to head straight for the beach resorts. This is a shame because its Old Town *(see pp12–13)* quarter is a particularly enchanting ensemble of centuries-old architecture and fine museums. Among them is the former convent of Nossa Senhora da Assunção, which houses the excellent archaeological museum.

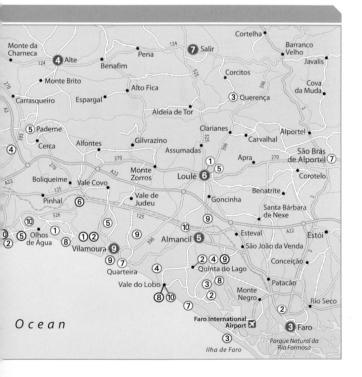

THE CAROB BEAN

The versatile carob bean tree is found throughout the Caldeirão mountain region. The beans are sometimes used as animal feed but also as a chocolate substitute. Pods can be ground and mixed with wheat flour to make tasty black bread. The gum is used in the textile and pharmaceutical industries.

4 Alte
MAP H3

Described as "a delightful snapshot of the real Algarve" in many a tourist brochure, Alte is indeed a picture of beauty and serenity. The little village with its whitewashed façades, cobbled streets, filigree chimney pots and rural charm appears to have little time for the 21st century, but always greets visitors with a warm handshake and a ready smile. The central attraction is the picnic spot near the stream. The area is also renowned for its handicrafts and colourful folklore.

Almancil
azulejo

5 Almancil
MAP J5

One of the most resplendent of all the Algarve's treasures is the 18th-century Igreja Matriz de São Lourenço *(see p22)*, just outside Almancil. Outstanding *azulejo* panels in the church depict episodes in the life of St Lawrence, while the highly ornate cupola is a breathtaking exercise in trompe l'oeil – indeed, some say it is the best example of its kind outside Rome.

6 Loulé

This cheerful market town *(see pp22–3)* is renowned as a centre of traditional handicrafts. The copper, leather and ceramic goods hammered out in the dozens of workshops dotted around its streets are some of the most sought after in the Algarve. These can be purchased at Loulé's bustling market *(see p77)*, along with an amazing selection of fruit and vegetables, fresh fish, herbs, cheeses, spices, honey, bottled liqueurs and sugared fig cakes. Loulé was an important Moorish settlement, and remnants of Muslim rule still exist.

7 Salir
MAP J3

In springtime, wild flowers of every hue blanket the meadows around this hilltop hamlet, with its ruined 12th-century Moorish castle *(see p44)* and small museum. The terraced battlements are now reclaimed to ingenious effect by enterprising locals who use them as vegetable plots. The short walk around the castle foundations is rewarded with an inviting panorama over the limestone massif of Rocha da Pena. The area is a well-known nesting site for the huge eagle owl. Naturalists may also be lucky enough to spy a common genet or an Egyptian mongoose.

8 Portimão

Portimão's *(see pp38–9)* esplanade is lined with pretty gardens and a variety of restaurants and cafés. This is the departure point for sightseeing cruises along the Arade River; it is also the location of the excellent Museu de Portimão *(see p47)*. Nearby are the Autódromo Internacional do Algarve, a world-class racing track, and Ocean Revival Park, a unique artificial reef made of sunken warships, perfect for diving.

Castle of São João, near Ferragudo

9 Vilamoura
MAP H5

With its glamorous reputation, Vilamoura is the resort choice for yachters and the jet set. The boardwalk is also the jumping-off point for coastal cruises on graceful schooners. The region as a whole is of great environmental and historical significance – the wetland surrounding the resort is a protected nature reserve, and the Museu Cerro da Vila (see p46) is one of the most important Roman sites in Portugal.

Marina at Vilamoura

10 Ferragudo
MAP E5

Ferragudo has admirably managed to avoid the more garish trappings of tourism and looks better for it. Sitting at the mouth of the Rio Arade, this attractive fishing village tumbles down to a busy little quayside bristling with fishermen's huts, artisan's workshops and one or two truly memorable seafood restaurants (see p89). The maze of steep alleys lead up to a handsome church. Praia Grande is a generous swathe of sand, which is popular sunbathing territory, and also the location of a big windsurfing school.

A TOUR OF VILLAGES

MORNING

An ideal starting point for your drive is **Loulé** on a Saturday morning, to take advantage of the bustling market. An early start will ensure you get the best choice of the produce. Aim to arrive at about 9am and allow an hour for browsing the stalls.

Order a coffee in Café Calcinha (Praça da República 67) before jumping in the car and heading north on the N396 to the quaint hamlet of **Querença** (see p84) with its whitewashed church and ancient stone cross. Take time to soak up the rural atmosphere, perhaps over a snack, at one of the cafés overlooking the square.

Head north for **Salir** on the M510, a meandering drive that weaves through verdant woodland, before turning west on the N124. Explore the castle ruins and admire the superb views of the **Rocha da Pena** limestone plateau. If you have arrived on a weekday, the little archaeological museum next to the castle will be open.

AFTERNOON

Continue on the N124 to **Alte** for lunch, perhaps at one of the traditional cafés located near the church. Then allow an hour to explore one of the Algarve's prettiest villages and shop for traditional handicrafts.

End the afternoon by continuing to **Paderne** (see p84), reached by travelling west on the N124 and then south on the N270. Follow the signs to visit the 12th-century Moorish castle (see p44).

See map on pp80–81

Other Villages and Sights

1 Estômbar
MAP E4

From this village follow the signs to Sítio das Fontes and discover a delightful hideaway picnic spot overlooking the Arade river. An old watermill can be seen among the beautiful surroundings.

Capela de Nossa Senhora da Rocha

2 Forte e Capela de Nossa Senhora da Rocha
MAP F5

Perched on a promontory, the tiny 15th-century chapel of Our Lady of the Rock is noted for its unusual octagonal cupola. The clifftop views take in eccentric rock formations and a beautiful golden beach.

3 Querença
MAP K4

A charming, hill-top hamlet slumbering in isolated beauty and crowned by the simple Igreja Nossa Senhora da Assunção.

4 Barragem do Arade
MAP F3

Birdsong echoes around this huge, picturesque reservoir, which makes a wonderful picnic spot. The rolling countryside is great hiking and mountain-biking territory.

5 Paderne
MAP G4

A world away from the villas and beaches of the Algarve coast. Paderne's faded, timeworn charm is mirrored in the village by some lovely 19th-century buildings. Several friendly café-restaurants dotted around the vicinity provide welcome refreshment.

6 São Bartolomeu de Messines
MAP G3

Poet João de Deus (1830–96) is synonymous with this quiet rural town. The church has some amazing twisted sandstone pillars, which are unique in the Algarve.

7 Calçadinha Roman Road
MAP D4 ▪ Interpretation
Centre: Rua do Matadouro 2, São Brás de Alportel; (289) 840 004; 9.30am–1pm & 2–5.30pm Tue–Sat

The Calçadinha, or cobbled street, is 1,480 m (4,855 ft) in length. It was part of the region's Roman road network and can still be walked.

8 Praia do Carvoeiro
MAP E5

This picturesque beach is wedged between steep-sided cliffs and is framed by rows of holiday apartments and restaurants. It is a popular haunt for families in the summer, and for golfers during the winter months.

9 Alcantarilha
MAP F4

A village known for its gruesome bone chapel, with the skeletal remains of 1,500 former parishioners covering the ceilings and walls.

10 Alcalar
MAP D4

The Alcalar burial chambers (see p38) are a series of Megalithic tombs. The drive here is a delight in itself, passing through rows of ancient oak and olive trees.

Beaches

1 Praia da Galé, Armação de Pêra
MAP F5

Two half-moons of smooth white sand make up this beach, interrupted only by some unusual outcrops of ochre-splashed sandstone.

2 Praia da Oura, Albufeira
MAP G5

Located at the bottom of "The Strip", this is a hugely popular beach in summer, and attractive too, with its patches of yellow sandstone rock.

3 Praia de Faro, Ilha de Faro
MAP J6–K6

One of the narrow barrier islands that shelter the Ria Formosa lagoon, this giant sand spit is a magnet for Faro residents, and for those visitors wishing to escape the city heat.

4 Praia da Rocha, Portimão
MAP E4

One of the most famous beaches in the Algarve, this impressive swathe of golden sand stretches out in front of russet-coloured cliffs.

5 Praia de São Rafael, Albufeira
MAP G5

Some extraordinary rock formations protrude from the shallows of this pretty bay, fringed with fine sand.

Beachgoers at Praia dos Pescadores

6 Praia dos Pescadores, Albufeira
MAP G5

This beach is named for the colourful fishing boats that between use, were once left on the sand (see p36). The vessels now moor up in the marina.

7 Praia da Senhora da Rocha
MAP F5

Warm, clear waters lap this inviting envelope of sand, framed between high cliffs. The beach is overlooked by the chapel, Forte e Capela de Nossa Senhora da Rocha.

8 Praia da Falésia, Olhos de Água
MAP H5

A long, narrow beach that never gets too crowded, even in summer. It is exposed to fresh southwesterly winds, which attracts the windsurfing set. A good option if you are in search of some peace and quiet.

9 Praia de Vilamoura
MAP H5

The beach at Vilamoura enjoys an enviable location right next to the resort. Its waters are calmed by the harbour breakwater, and the place is often used as a backdrop by fashion photographers.

10 Praia de Vale do Lobo
MAP J5

This select beachfront is patronized by guests staying at the nearby Vale do Lobo resort. There are some excellent bar-cafés close by.

Rock formations at Praia de São Rafael

See map on pp80–81

Golf Courses

Panoramic view of the Pine Cliffs golf course

1 Pine Cliffs
MAP G5 ■ Praia da Falésia, Albufeira ■ (289) 500 113

This 9-hole, par 33 clifftop course is set against a spectacular Atlantic Ocean backdrop. The last hole is named "Devil's Parlour" (see p60).

2 San Lorenzo
MAP J5 ■ Quinta do Lago ■ (289) 396 522

This magnificent, 18-hole, par 72 course is considered by World Golf magazine to be one of Europe's top five golf courses (see p60).

3 Quinta do Lago South
MAP J5 ■ Almancil ■ (289) 390 705

Quinta do Lago South, a famous championship course, has hosted the Portuguese Open several times. It is notable for four challenging par 5 holes (see p61).

4 Vale do Lobo
MAP J5 ■ Almancil ■ (289) 353 465

The Royal Course incorporates the world-famous par 3 16th hole with an extensive carry over cliffs (see p60). The Ocean Course follows an undulating layout.

5 Vilamoura Golf Courses
MAP H5 ■ Vilamoura ■ (289) 310 333

The Old Course, Pinhal, Laguna, Millennium and Victoria (see p60) are 18-hole, par 72 layouts, in beautifully landscaped settings.

6 Amendoeira Faldo & O'Connor Jnr
MAP F5 ■ Amendoeira Golf Resort, EN 529, Alcântarilha ■ (289) 310 333

The Amendoeira Golf Resort has two acclaimed 18-hole layouts – designed by golfers Sir Nick Faldo and Christy O'Connor Jnr.

7 Vale da Pinta Course, Pestana Carvoeiro
MAP E5 ■ Pestana Golf & Resort, Carvoeiro ■ (282) 340 900

An ancient olive tree spreads over one of the greens of the 18-hole Pinta course, while the 18-hole Gramacho layout has some heavily bunkered greens.

8 Pinheiros Altos
MAP J5 ■ Quinta do Lago ■ (289) 359 910

An independent 27-hole, par 72 course built on the Quinta do Lago estate, embracing part of the Parque Natural da Ria Formosa.

9 Vila Sol Golf
MAP H5 ■ Morgadinhos, Vilamoura ■ (289) 320 370

Known for its water hazards, this 27-hole, par 72 course is a challenge for golfers of all handicap levels.

10 Balaia Golf
MAP G5 ■ Albufeira ■ (289) 570 200

This executive 9-hole, par 27 course (see p61) is built on undulating terrain, punctuated with umbrella pine and cork oak trees.

Places to Shop

① Loulé Market
MAP J4 ▪ Praça da República, Loulé ▪ Open 7am–3pm Mon–Sat
This market sells fruit and vegetables, fish, herbs, spices, cheeses, flowers and local handicrafts (see p75).

② Forum Algarve Shopping Centre
MAP K6 ▪ EN 125, Sítio das Figuras, Faro ▪ Open 10am–midnight daily
With an architectural design inspired by Faro's historical centre, this is the region's biggest shopping mall (see p74).

③ Algarve Shopping Centre
MAP G4 ▪ EN 125, Guia ▪ Open 10am–midnight daily
A modern mall with national and international chains, a cinema and a food hall (see p74).

④ Quinta Shopping Mall
MAP J5 ▪ Quinta do Lago ▪ Open 10am–7pm daily (to midnight Jul & Aug)
An elegant open-air mall with several designer boutiques, sports outlets and restaurants (see p74).

⑤ Sardinha
MAP J4 ▪ Largo D. Pedro I, 3, Loulé ▪ (289) 512 936 ▪ Open 10am–7pm Mon–Fri (to 3pm on Sat); Closed Sun
The humble sardine is just one source of inspiration for the many souvenirs sold at this quirky studio.

⑥ Quinta do Morgado da Torre Vineyard
MAP E4 ▪ Penina, near Alvor ▪ Open 10am–noon & 2–5pm Mon–Fri
Visit the retail outlet of this vineyard and splash out on a bottle of Tapada da Torre – one of the best wines in the Algarve (see p69).

⑦ Quarteira Fish Market
MAP H5 ▪ Largo do Peixe, Quarteira ▪ Open 8:30am–1:30pm Mon–Sat
The most famous market (see p74) of its kind on the south coast; arrive early for the best choice of fish and seafood. Superb value for money makes this popular with restaurateurs, as well as with the public.

Urn, Porches Pottery

⑧ Porches Pottery
MAP F4 ▪ EN 125, Porches, Lagoa ▪ Open 9am–6pm Mon–Fri, 10am–2pm Sat
One of the first commercial ceramic outlets (see p75) in the region. The glazed pottery and earthenware goods are produced in-house.

⑨ Gigagarden
MAP G4 ▪ Guia, EN 125 ▪ Open 9am–7:30pm Mon–Sat, 10am–7pm Sun
This sprawling garden centre displays a variety of shrubs, trees and cacti.

⑩ Apolónia Supermarket
MAP J5 ▪ Avenida 5 de Outubro, 271, Almancil ▪ Open 8am–8pm daily (summer: to 9pm)
The best supermarket in the country for imported produce that is difficult to buy elsewhere in Portugal.

The bakery at Apolónia Supermarket

See map on pp80–81

Nightlife

① Vilamoura Marina
MAP H5

A multitude of bars, eateries and late-night shopping. The spectacular firework displays here round off many a long summer evening.

② Vilamoura Casino
MAP H5 ▪ Praça do Casino, Vilamoura ▪ Open 7pm–3am daily

Sophisticated gaming room with baccarat, Portuguese dice, roulette, blackjack and 500 big-jackpot slot machines. The Miralago Room stages world-class music and dance.

③ The JailHouse, Carvoeiro
MAP E5 ▪ Rua do Escondadinho 9, Praia do Carvoeiro ▪ Open 6pm–1am daily

Known as Sob e Desce in the 1960s, when it hosted the likes of Cat Stevens, this iconic entertainment venue is still appreciated by holiday-makers and locals alike.

④ Avenida Tomás Cabreira, Praia da Rocha
MAP E5

In one of the first tourist resorts in the Algarve (see p39), this long esplanade is crammed with funky bars and nightclubs.

A lively street in Albufeira

⑤ Le Club Santa Eulália, Albufeira
MAP G5 ▪ Praia de Santa Eulália ▪ (289) 598 070 ▪ Open midnight–6am Fri & Sat; restaurant: 8pm–midnight Tue–Sat

Contemporary interior design and a generous dance floor characterize this fashionable nightspot (see p67).

Spacious dancefloor at Kadoc

⑥ Kadoc, Vilamoura
MAP H5 ▪ Cerca da Areia, near Vilamoura ▪ Open from midnight Sat–Mon

The biggest club (see p67) in the Algarve attracts thousands of revellers to its summer parties.

⑦ Katedral, Praia da Rocha
MAP E5 ▪ Avenida Tomás Cabreira, Praia da Rocha ▪ Open summer: 1–6am Wed & Thu, 1–7am Sat & Sun

A sprawling popular late-night dance venue (see p67) catering for a range of musical tastes.

⑧ Gecko Club, Vale do Lobo
MAP J5 ▪ The Square (Praça) ▪ Open Apr–Sep: 11–5am ▪ Closed Oct–Mar

This club boasts a sleek and modern interior and a wide choice of cocktails.

⑨ Melting Pot, Quinta do Lago
MAP J5 ▪ Lote 27 Quinta Shopping ▪ Open 10–2am daily

A popular English-pub-style bar and restaurant heaving with locals, expatriates and tourists.

⑩ Kiss, Albufeira
MAP G5 ▪ Rua Vasco da Gama, Albufeira ▪ Open summer: 2–7am daily (from 11pm Thu)

Possibly the best-known nightclub (see p66) in Portugal, attracting a mixed 20-something crowd.

Places to Eat

PRICE CATEGORIES

For a three-course meal for one with half
a bottle of wine (or equivalent meal),
taxes and extra charges.

€ under €30 ■ €€ €30–€50 ■ €€€ over €50

1 Ramires, Guia
MAP G4 ■ Rua 25 de Abril, Guia
■ (289) 561 232 ■ No veg dishes ■ €

Diners have been frequenting this
restaurant since 1964 for the best
chicken piri-piri in the Algarve.

2 Gusto, Conrad Resort
MAP J5 ■ Conrad Algarve Hotel
& Resort, Estrada do Quinta do Lago
■ (289) 350 700 ■ Open 7:30–10:30pm
Wed–Sun ■ Closed Jan & Feb ■ €€

Consultant chef Heinz Beck is behind
this first-class gourmet dining venue,
which has a Michelin star to its name.

3 Restaurante Evaristo, Albufeira
MAP G5 ■ Praia do Evaristo ■ (289)
591 666 ■ Closed Dec & Jan ■ No
veg dishes ■ €€

This chic beachfront eatery has great
ocean views. Enjoy seafood alfresco.

4 Veneza, Paderne
MAP G4 ■ Estrada de Paderne
560a ■ (289) 367 129 ■ Closed 15–31
May & 15–31 Oct ■ No veg dishes ■ €

A rural eatery famed for its rustic,
menu and vast selection of wine.

5 Vila Joya, Albufeira
MAP F5 ■ Praia da Galé, Estrada
da Galé, Albufeira ■ (289) 591 795
■ Thu–Tue ■ Reservations required
■ www.vilajoya.com ■ €€€

Set on the Atlantic coast, this restaurant serves gourmet food with
a wine list to match.

6 O Barradas, Silves
MAP F4 ■ Venda Nova,
Palmeirinha ■ (282) 443 308
■ D only; closed Wed & Dec ■ €

Succulent meat, fresh fish and great
service ensure a memorable dinner.

7 Casa Velha, Quinta do Lago
MAP J5 ■ Quinta do Lago ■ (289)
394 983 ■ Visa & Amex only ■ D only
■ Closed Sun, Oct–May: Mon, mid-
Dec–Feb ■ Reservations required
■ No veg dishes ■ €€€

Mentioned in the celebrated Michelin
Guide, this restaurant serves French
cuisine with a Mediterranean twist.

8 Sueste, Ferragudo
MAP E5 ■ Rua da Ribeira 91
■ (282) 461 592 ■ Closed Sun & Jan
■ No veg dishes ■ €€

Known for its range of seafood
dishes, Sueste has its best tables on
the quayside. The interior is set in a
traditional Algarvian fishing cottage.

9 A Quinta, Almancil
MAP J5 ■ Rua Vale Formosa
■ (289) 393 357 ■ D only (Fri L & D);
closed Sun, Mon; mid-Dec–Jan ■ €€€

An imaginative menu features
dishes such as sea bass with crunchy
mangetout and spicy Thai curry
sauce. Vegetarians are catered for.

10 O Charneco, Estômbar
MAP E4 ■ Rua Joaquim Manuel
Charneco 3 ■ (282) 431 113 ■ D only;
closed Sun & Jan ■ No credit cards
■ No veg dishes ■ €

There is no menu here. Diners at this
lively and traditional restaurant enjoy
a daily selection of seven courses of
tasty regional fare, accompanied by
a bottle of the house wine.

O Charneco, Estômbar

See map on pp80–81

TOP 10 Eastern Region

Long, narrow sandbank islands stretch along much of the coastline of the eastern Algarve (Sotavento). These natural barriers shelter a fragile lagoon ecosystem that is home to a staggering variety of flora and fauna. Tucked behind them are time-worn fishing villages and hamlets. Further east, beautiful Renaissance churches loom over picturesque towns and elegant cities, replete with Roman bridges, Moorish castles and the distinctive pyramid-shaped rooflines. The sparse interior is Nature's preserve, underlined by a culture and heritage that has remained unchanged for centuries.

Azulejos at Estói

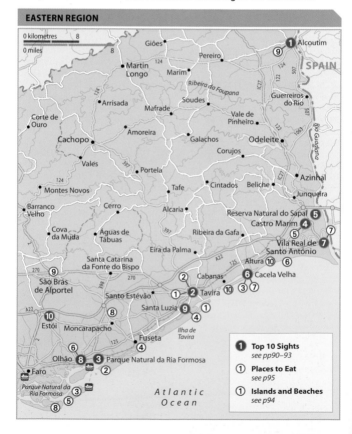

EASTERN REGION

0 kilometres 8
0 miles 8

Giões
Pereiro
Martin Longo
Marim
Ribeira da Foupana
1 Alcoutim **9**
SPAIN
Guerreiros do Rio
Arrisada
Mafrade
Soudes
Vale de Pinheiro
Corte de Ouro
Amoreira
Galachos
Odeleite
Cachopo
Corujos
Rio Guadiana
Valés
Portela
Azinhal
Montes Novos
Tafe
Cintados
Beliche
Junqueira
Barranco Velho
Cerro
Alcaria
Reserva Natural do Sapal **5**
Castro Marim **4**
Cova da Muda
Águas de Tábuas
Ribeira da Gafa
5
7
Santa Catarina da Fonte do Bispo
Eira da Palma
Vila Real de Santo António **7**
São Brás de Alportel **9**
Altura **10** **6**
Cabanas **2**
Cacela Velha **6**
Santo Estévão
Tavira **1** **2** **10** **3** **7**
Estói **10**
Santa Luzia **9** **1**
Moncarapacho
Ilha de Tavira
Fuseta **4**
Olhão **8** **3** **2** Parque Natural da Ria Formosa
Faro
Parque Natural da Ria Formosa **3** **5**
8
Atlantic Ocean

1 Top 10 Sights
see pp90–93

1 Places to Eat
see p95

1 Islands and Beaches
see p94

1 Alcoutim
MAP P1 ■ Castle: 10am–1pm &
2–7pm daily (winter: to 6pm) ■ Adm

The ramparts of a 14th-century castle (see p44) still stand vigil over this delightful riverside hamlet (see p55) that nestles on the upper reaches of the River Guadiana. On the Spanish side, the slumbering village of Sanlúcar de Guadiana amounts to a mirror image of Alcoutim. Once upon a time these two neighbours were at war with each other, and it was in the castle that a short-lived peace treaty was signed in 1371. A ferry now regularly shuttles between the two villages. Another way to cross the river is by zip line (see p57).

2 Tavira
Churches are symbolic of Tavira (see pp16–17), with nearly 40 towers and spires piercing the town's skyline. Two are of great historical significance: the Igreja da Misericórdia, the Algarve's most important Renaissance monument; and the Igreja de Santa Maria do Castelo, the final resting place of Dom Paio Peres Correia, who helped to retake Portugal from the Moors. The elegant Roman bridge spanning the River Gilão is another landmark that lends character to a town considered by many to be the most charming in the region.

The famous clockface of Igreja de Santa Maria do Castelo in Tavira

Parque Natural da Ria Formosa

3 Parque Natural da Ria Formosa
This vast realm of marshland, salinas and sand-dune islands is home to an incredible assortment of wildlife (see pp30–33). The lagoon habitat is one of the most important wetland zones in Europe. The park's headquarters are near Olhão. Three exciting nature trails, São Lourenço, Quinta do Lago and Olhão, provide excellent opportunities for observing wildlife at close quarters.

4 Castro Marim
MAP P3

The time-worn frontier town of Castro Marim looms with genteel poise over the mouth of the River Guadiana, and its twin castles bear witness to the strategic importance that the settlement played during centuries past. Grand views from the ramparts of the main 13th-century stronghold (see p45) encompass the Reserva Natural do Sapal to the north and Vila Real de Santo António to the south. Spain shimmers in the distance.

5 Reserva Natural do Sapal
MAP P4 ■ www.natural.pt

Much of this wetland park comprises working salt pans, but it is also a major winter feeding ground for spoonbill, greater flamingo, Kentish plover, avocet and other birds. The visitor centre (closed Sat and Sun) is on the edge of the salt marsh, and there is a lovely nature trail (see p57).

The fortress at Cacela Velha

6 Cacela Velha
MAP N4

Thought to have been a Phoenician settlement in origin, this quaint coastal hamlet commands one of the most unspoiled locations in the Algarve. A patchwork of fields and meadows surround a bluff crowned by an 18th-century fortress. Lying in its shadow is the parish church; its whitewashed candescence plays off the façades of the fishermen's cottages lining the tiny square.

7 Vila Real de Santo António
MAP P4

The original settlement here was submerged by monstrous tidal surges in the early 17th century. It was reborn in the late 18th century, when the Marquês de Pombal designed a new town based on the Lisbon grid system. The town now attracts Spanish daytrippers from Ayamonte, just over the River Guadiana, which in turn is a magnet for sightseers from Portugal.

8 Olhão
MAP L5

One of the liveliest fishing ports in the Algarve, Olhão has some fine seafood restaurants. The whole town revolves around fishing, a fact exemplified by the 17th-century parish church, built with donations from the local fishermen. At the chapel of Nossa Senhora dos Aflitos, locals pray for the safe return of their loved ones during bad weather. The town's cube-shaped houses, with flat roof terraces and external staircases, reflect the close trade links once enjoyed with North Africa.

9 Santa Luzia
MAP M5

Stunted palmeiras, swaying lazily in the sea breezes, stud Santa Luzia's long esplanade. The village is synonymous with octopus, and dozens of empty *covos* (octopus pots) can be seen stacked near the quay, the hapless contents of which are probably on a dinner table. Summer sea safaris depart from the quayside and cruise the waters off Ilha de Tavira.

Fishing boats in Santa Luzia

PLUCKY PEOPLE OF OLHÃO

In 1808, Olhão staged an uprising against the French garrison, which was the catalyst for Napoleon's retreat from Portuguese soil. In order to transmit the good news to King João VI in Brazil, a group of Olhão fishermen sailed to Rio de Janeiro, bereft of navigational charts. Their incredible voyage across the Atlantic so impressed the king that upon his return to the throne he elevated Olhão to town status.

Statue, Palácio do Visconde de Estói

⑩ Estói

MAP K5 ■ Milreu Roman Ruins: May–Sep: 9:30am–1pm & 2–6:30pm Tue–Sun; Oct–Apr: 9am–1pm & 2–5:30pm Tue–Sun; adm

The inland village of Estói basks in the glory of two major attractions: Palácio do Visconde de Estói (see p54) and the Roman ruins at nearby Milreu. The renovated 19th-century palace retains its pink Rococo façade and period architecture. Twenty minutes' walk away, the well-preserved Roman ruins include a peristyle villa built in the 2nd century AD, with baths decorated with fish mosaics and a temple.

A DRIVE TO ALCOUTIM

▶ MORNING

A morning's drive north out of **Castro Marim** (see p91) on the EN122 will take you through undulating hills and lush valleys to the banks of the River Guadiana.

Allow a leisurely hour to reach **Alcoutim** (see p91). Ignore the IC27 highway; stay on the EN122 towards Junqueira and Azinhal. After 30 minutes you will see a sign for Alcoutim on the right. Ignore this. Instead, carry on past the Barragem de Odeleite reservoir and several small hamlets. You will reach a junction at Cruzamento. Turn right here towards Alcoutim.

Pause for a coffee at any one of the cafés in Praça da República before exploring the castle (see p44) and its museum. Afterwards, have lunch back in the square.

AFTERNOON

If it is a hot day, saunter over to **Praia Fluvial de Alcoutim** (see p94). Alternatively, catch the boat to neighbouring Spain and wander around Sanlúcar de Guadiana. Thrill seekers might want to return via the zip line (see p59).

To return to Castro Marim, follow the EN507 south out of Alcoutim along the banks of the Guadiana for one of the most inspiring drives in the Algarve. Stop by the ruins of the Villa Romana do Montinho das Laranjeiras, a 1st century AD Roman dwelling.

After Foz de Odeleite, the road returns to the hills before joining the EN122 and heading south.

See map on p90

Islands and Beaches

① Ilha de Tavira
MAP M5

A huge offshore sandbank stretching 11 km (7 miles) west from Tavira, connected to land by a 10-minute ferry from Quatro Águas. Alternatively, a mini railway can take you there from the resort of Pedras d'el Rei.

② Ilha da Armona
MAP L5–6

Popular with independent travellers, the beaches facing inland are served by bars and restaurants. A ferry from Olhão takes 15 minutes.

③ Ilha da Culatra
MAP L6

The beaches here enjoy splendid isolation, and nude sunbathing in the dunes is not uncommon. The ferry takes 45 minutes from Olhão.

④ Ilha da Fuseta
MAP M5

You can walk onto this island at low tide. The beaches are exquisite, and the waters of the lagoon provide a popular destination for windsurfers.

⑤ Praia do Farol
MAP L6

A beautiful sweep of sand on the bank of a long island. Farol can be reached by taking a 45-minute ferry ride from the Porta Nova wharf below Faro's Old Town district. There are also regular departures from Olhão.

Tranquil Praia do Farol

⑥ Praia Verde
MAP P4

One of several beaches that follow the yawning curve of Monte Gordo Bay, the "green beach" is named after a verdant umbrella pine forest that fringes the sand.

⑦ Praia de Cacela Velha
MAP N4

Overlooked by the tiny Fortaleza Cacela Velha (see p45), this secluded lagoon-fringed stretch of sand is perfect for sunbathing.

⑧ Ilha da Barreta
MAP K6

Boat departures from Faro's Porta Nova wharf shuttle visitors to this "deserted island", where wildlife can be observed. A bar-restaurant, O Estaminé, provides sustenance.

⑨ Praia Fluvial de Alcoutim
MAP P1

Known locally as Pego Fundo, this slither of sand fringing a tributary of the Guadiana is the only river beach in the Algarve.

⑩ Praia da Ilha de Cabanas
MAP N4

Less crowded than some of its neighbours, Cabanas' pristine beaches (see p49) lie in peaceful seclusion, and are reached by continuing westwards along the shores of Praia de Manta Rota.

Places to Eat

PRICE CATEGORIES

For a three-course meal for one with half a bottle of wine (or equivalent meal), taxes and extra charges.

....

€ under €30 ■ €€ €30–€50 ■ €€€ over €50

1 Brisa do Rio, Tavira
MAP M5 ■ Rua João Vaz Côrte Real 38 ■ (915) 434 452 ■ D only ■ Closed Wed & Nov ■ €

A regional dining hot spot, book in advance to secure a table at this acclaimed eatery.

2 A Ver Tavira, Tavira
MAP M4 ■ Calçada de Galeria, Tavira ■ (281) 381 363 ■ €€

A trendy eatery next to the castle with tapas and a *menú de dégustación*. Booking is essential.

3 Casa Velha, Cacela Velha
MAP N4 ■ Cacela Velha ■ (281) 952 297 ■ Closed Mon & Jan ■ No veg dishes ■ €

Set in a pretty hamlet, this quaint restaurant attracts an enthusiastic clientele for its *feijoada de longueirão* (razor clams in bean stew), oysters and other seafood dishes.

4 Marisqueira O Capelo, Santa Luzia
MAP M5 ■ Avenida Eng. Duarte Pacheco 40, Santa Luzia ■ (281) 381 670 ■ Closed Tue D, Wed & Jan ■ No veg dishes ■ €€

At a table on the terrace is the best way to savour this classic fish and seafood restaurant. Specialities include tuna stew and octopus rice.

5 A Tasca Medieval, Castro Marim
MAP P3 ■ Rua 25 de Abril 65 ■ (281) 513 196 ■ Closed Tue ■ No veg dishes ■ €

Top-notch food is served at this traditional restaurant. The house speciality *açorda de galinha* (bread-based chicken stew) must be ordered in advance, but it is worth the wait.

6 Restaurante Ria Formosa, Olhão
MAP L5 ■ Avenida 5 de Outubro 14 ■ (289) 702 504 ■ Closed Thu ■ No veg dishes ■ €

One local describes this much-loved restaurant as "an ocean under one roof". The menu bursts with catches, such as fresh *besugos* (mullet).

7 Os Arcos, Vila Real
MAP P4 ■ Avenida da República 45, Vila Real de Santo António ■ (281) 543 764 ■ €

A large, cavernous seafood restaurant on the town's riverfront.

Stylish interior at À Terra

8 À Terra, Moncarapacho
MAP L5 ■ Vila Monte Farm House, Sítio dos Caliços, Moncarapacho ■ (289) 790 790 ■ €€

Locally-sourced produce and herbs from the garden are used to prepare delicious meals, with a distinctly Mediterranean flavour.

9 Luís dos Frangos, São Brás de Alportel
MAP K4 ■ Rua Dr José Dias Sanchos 134, São Brás de Alportel ■ (289) 842 635 ■ Closed Mon and last 2 weeks Sep ■ No veg dishes ■ €

A down-to-earth eatery that serves up grilled chicken to tourists and locals.

10 A Chaminé, Altura
MAP N4 ■ Avenida 24 de Junho, Altura ■ (281) 950 100 ■ Closed Tue except Jul–Aug & 3rd week of Nov ■ €€

Noted by Michelin, particularly for its fish and seafood menu, this traditional restaurant is pleasant and homely.

See map on p90 ➤

TOP 10 Western Region

The Western Algarve (Barlavento) blends a precipitous Atlantic coastline with a green Mediterranean interior. The wild, windblown promontories associated with the legend of Henry the Navigator yield to forest-clad hills and cloud-tipped mountains. Some of the region's most spectacular beaches nestle on the south coast under outcrops of ochre-splashed rock. Underpinning all this is a rich historical thread of Baroque churches and Manueline chapels, stark sea defences and baffling Neolithic monuments. Visitor attractions abound, with quaint restaurants in hushed villages waiting to be discovered, and lively resorts with a more cosmopolitan flavour.

Windmill, Odeceixe

WESTERN REGION

1 Top 10 Sights
  see pp99–101

1 Places to Eat
  see p105

1 Places to Shop
  see p104

1 Beaches
  see p102

1 Watersports
  see p103

Previous pages Praia do Camillo, Lagos

The natural sea caves at Ponta da Piedade near Lagos

1 Lagos

One of the most popular resort towns in southern Portugal, Lagos *(see pp26–9)* immediately captures the imagination with its carefree holiday spirit, laid-back lifestyle and immense historical wealth. Its greatest treasure is the Igreja de Santo António. The nearby beaches are equally attractive, with their fine golden sand, ochre-splashed cliffs and bizarre outcrops of sandstone pillars.

2 Monchique and Caldas de Monchique

Monchique *(see pp20–21)*, a rustic little market town, is tucked away in the forested Serra de Monchique under a mantle of towering eucalyptus and magnolia. Nestling in its shadow is Caldas de Monchique, a charming leafy hamlet glowing in the fame of its renowned spa facility, where the sparkling mineral water is endowed with some remarkable curative properties. The Serra's unique Mediterranean-Atlantic habitat is a haven for wildlife. Sweeping views from Fóia and Picota crown this hugely diverse and fertile area.

3 Sagres

Sagres' claim to fame is the huge landmark fort spread across the arm of the precipitous Ponta de Sagres. It is here that Henry the Navigator's original fortress and the Vila do Infante – his legendary school of navigation – is said to have been located. Little remains of either

except for perhaps the giant pebble Rosa dos Ventos (wind compass) and the plain little chapel of Nossa Senhora da Graça, both supposedly used by Henry in the 15th century. Sagres *(see pp34–5)* itself is a modest town bestowed with a pretty harbour and some magnificent beaches that attract surfers from around the globe.

Nossa Senhora da Graça in Sagres

4 Raposeira

MAP B5 ▪ EN 125, Raposeira ▪ Chapel: Open May–Sep: 10:30am–1pm & 2–6:30pm, Oct–Apr: 9am–1pm & 2–5:30pm; closed Mon; adm

The main attraction, located 1 km (half a mile) east of this small village, is the 14th-century chapel Nossa Senhora de Guadalupe, thought to be one of the oldest examples of Gothic architecture in the Algarve. Henry the Navigator was said to have prayed here when he lived in Raposeira, as did many a crew before departing for unknown lands. Inside the chapel, built in honour of the Virgin of Guadalupe, enigmatic stone heads peer down from the ceiling.

The cliffs of Cabo de São Vicente

5 Cabo de São Vicente
MAP B5

An austere landscape, dramatic limestone cliffs and a restless, unforgiving sea led Greek chroniclers to describe this windblown cape as the end of the earth. The Romans revered the rocky outcrop and called it Promontorium Sacrum, a place where the setting sun hissed in its dying embers as the ocean swallowed it up. The promontory retains an air of mystique. Henry the Navigator is said to have had a house in the small castle to the right of the lighthouse.

6 Parque Natural do Sudoeste Alentejano e Costa Vicentina
MAP B3–5 & C3 ■ Park headquarters: Rua Serpa Pinto 32, Odemira, Alentejo; (283) 322 735

The entire coastline of the western Algarve lies within the boundaries of this wild and rocky nature reserve. Dozens of scarce and endemic plant species thrive here – it is a botanist's paradise. Hundreds of different species of birdlife *(see p59)* flutter and glide above the coastal plains, while, not surprisingly, ornithologists gather with binoculars primed.

7 Barragem da Bravura
MAP D4

The huge, man-made lake 10 km (6 miles) north of Lagos is a wonderful place at which to unpack the picnic hamper. In spring, fields of orchids nestle under delicate umbrellas of almond blossom, with butterflies flitting from bloom to bloom. Towering eucalyptus encroach upon the lakeside, and the woods are a favourite haunt of red foxes and wild boar. The higher ground north of the dam is generously wooded with cork oak, and it is from this area that the best views of the lake can be enjoyed.

8 Odeceixe
MAP C1 ■ Windmill: Open Jun–Sep: 9am–noon & 2–6pm Tue–Sat

The River Seixe meanders past this pretty little village, which makes a handy base for surfers who are keen to ride the big swells that thunder onto Odeceixe beach. A lone windmill sitting above the village used to take advantage of the fresh winds whipped up by the Atlantic in days gone by. Today it is a popular vantage point for scanning the Alentejo countryside. This sleepy backwater is about as far

Parque Natural do Sudoeste Alentejano e Costa Vicentina

as you can get from the summer throngs that pack the coastal resorts. The good-value guesthouses found here fill up fast during the summer.

9 Vila do Bispo
MAP B4 ▪ Menhir Circuit, Hortas do Tabual, Vila do Bispo

The landscape around Vila do Bispo is rich with evidence of the Algarve's prehistoric past (see p57). Mysterious menhirs, also known as megaliths, dot the countryside. Near Hortas do Tabual, a number of these stones, some bearing crudely carved crosses, appear to form a circle. Archaeologists speculate that this could be the site of the mythical Church of the Raven, supposedly where the remains of St Vincent were interred before being taken to Lisbon.

Aerial view of Aljezur town

10 Aljezur
MAP C3

The humble ruins of a 10th-century Moorish castle (see p44) stand sentinel-like over a higgledy-piggledy collection of whitewashed houses and café-restaurants that constitute the village of Aljezur. A steep, cobbled path leads up to the time-worn but sturdy castle walls and the splendid view beyond. This riverine area was once a breeding ground for malaria-carrying mosquitoes, and in the 18th century some of the villagers were persuaded to relocate to Igreja Nova, Aljezur's "modern" counterpart to the east.

A TOUR OF THE WEST

▶ MORNING

Breakfast in **Lagos** (see p99) at the café in Praça Infante Dom Henrique near the castle walls, and then set out to explore the west coast.

The drive follows the EN125, crossing the boundary of the **Parque Natural do Sudoeste Alentejano e Costa Vicentina**. The road winds on – via the tiny 14th-century chapel of Nossa Senhora da Guadalupe and the prehistoric sights of **Vila do Bispo** – to **Sagres** (see p99) and its landmark 17th-century fort.

For an invigorating walk and to further appreciate the seascape at Sagres, follow the path around the promontory.

By now, it should be time for refreshments at Café-Restaurante Cochina on Praça da República. For something more substantial, try the Café-Restaurant Pau de Pita on Rua Comandante Matoso.

AFTERNOON

Sagres (see p99) has a pretty harbour, which can be investi-gated on foot. The nearby **Fortaleza de Sagres** (see p45), the supposed location of Henry the Navigator's famed academy, is definitely worthy of an hour-long exploration.

No trip to the west coast would be complete without a visit to **Cabo de São Vicente**, which is a short drive northwest. The clifftop vistas are truly awe-inspiring and offer a suitably dramatic way to end the day.

See map on p98 ←

Beaches

1 Praia do Amado, Carrapateira
MAP B4

One of the surfer's favourites *(see p48)*, Amado's Atlantic swells attract enthusiasts keen to ride the surf back into the wide sweeping beach.

Praia do Camilo, Lagos

2 Praia do Camilo, Lagos
MAP D5

A magical beach *(see p27)* and one of the most picturesque in the Algarve, Camilo *(see p48)* is framed by a collection of sandstone outcrops and a warren of caves and grottoes.

3 Praia de Odeceixe
MAP C1

The River Seixe runs into this delightfully secluded stretch of sand *(see p48)*, tucked away right up in the northern reaches of the Algarve.

4 Praia da Figueira, Figueira
MAP C5

Surrounded by tawny-hued cliffs, this beach is accessible only by foot, and can be reached by a narrow trail that meanders through a pretty valley.

5 Praia do Burgau
MAP C5

One of the best locations in the area for snorkelling and diving, the beach skirts Burgau resort and is hemmed in on either side by sloping cliffs.

6 Praia do Martinhal
MAP B6

A fabulous location for windsurfing, with the ocean lapping a golden swathe of sand. The beach is also conveniently situated near the town of Sagres.

7 Praia do Beliche, near Sagres
MAP B5

The steep climb down a cliff path to the beach is rewarded with a wonderfully secluded wedge of pristine sand. Due to its slightly awkward location, it does not tend to attract many visitors.

8 Praia da Luz
MAP C5

A fine beach, with very easy access to resort amenities, Praia da Luz can become crowded in high season. However, there is always some room, especially towards its eastern flank.

9 Praia de Monte Clérigo, Aljezur
MAP C2

Another beach preferred by the surfing set, and tourists that have a more independent spirit. This is a wild, isolated landscape with untamed breakers.

10 Meia Praia, Lagos
MAP D5

At 4 km (2 miles), this is one of the longest beaches *(see p49)* in the Algarve, allowing plenty of room for sunbathers to share the vista with water-skiers and windsurfers.

See map on p98

Watersports

1 **Diving**
MAP D5 ■ www.blue-ocean-divers.de

Explore caves, canyons, reefs and wrecks. Many schools also offer night dives, snorkelling safaris and PADI certification courses up to professional level.

2 **Windsurfing**
MAP D5 ■ www.algarve watersport.com

The reliable winds off Meia Praia allow windsurfers to hone their skills in an expanse of open water perfectly suited to this popular sport.

3 **Coasteering**
MAP B6 ■ www.coastline algarve.com

Cliff-climbing, swimming in caves and ambling along coastal paths – this is coasteering, an exhilarating way in which to explore the area between Lagos and Sagres.

4 **Kite Surfing**
MAP E5–L6 ■ www.extreme algarve.com

One minute you are surfing, the next you are airborne. The best season for this watersport is May–Oct, and the flatwater lagoons near Lagos and Alvor are ideal locations.

5 **Sailing**
MAP D5 ■ www.southwest trainingcenter.com

Sailing is ubiquitous in the Algarve, and there are plenty of schools in the region providing tuition. Cruise companies also charter yachts and organize sailing holidays.

6 **Big Game Fishing**
MAP D5 ■ www.pescamar.info

Several sports fishing operators are based in Marina de Lagos (see p27), and use boats with state-of-the-art tackle and a fighting chair to pursue shark and marlin.

7 **Paddleboarding**
MAP D5 ■ www.jahshaka surf.com

Standup paddleboarding is one of the more novel methods of exploring the coastline. Options include night-time tours using innovative underwater lighting systems.

8 **Water-skiing**
MAP C5 ■ www.beachhut watersports.com

Well sheltered from the wind, the waters off Praia da Luz provide an ideal arena in which to learn basic manoeuvres, practise wake crossings and try deep-water starts.

9 **Kayaking**
MAP D5 ■ www.kayak-lagos.com

Kayaking is a great way to see the grottoes and beaches around Lagos' beautiful Ponta da Piedade (see p26).

10 **Surfing**
MAP B3 ■ www.arrifana surfschool.com

West coast beaches such as Praia de Monte Clérigo and Praia do Castelejo are synonymous with surfing (see p57). There are also a wide range of surf camps and schools around.

Surfing at Praia da Arrifana

Places to Shop

Shoppers on Rua Cândido dos Reis

1 Rua Cândido dos Reis/ Rua 25 de Abril, Lagos

MAP D5

The two busiest streets in town, where shoppers can browse the rows of stores and boutiques for jewellery, handicrafts and fashion.

2 Casa dos Arcos

MAP E3 ■ José Salvador, Estrada Velha, Monchique

One of the few places in the Algarve where you can purchase *cadeiras de tesoura*, the traditional folding wooden chairs, which are hand-crafted to an ancient Roman design.

3 Mediconforto

MAP D5 ■ Rua Soeiro da Costa 26, Lagos

A handy health-food shop selling a huge selection of minerals, vitamins, homeopathic remedies and natural cosmetics.

4 Atelier Opalina

MAP D5 ■ Praça do Infante 1, Lagos

A stunning range of handmade jewellery fashioned out of gold, silver, mother-of-pearl, amber and precious stones.

5 Lagos Surf Center

MAP D5 ■ Rua Silva Lopes 31, Lagos ■ www.lagossurfcenter.com

An outlet for O'Neill, Rip Curl, Billabong and Quiksilver, you will find everything you need to surf here, including a choice of boards and beachwear. Staff can arrange rentals, surf schools and safaris, as well as accommodation.

6 Baptista Supermarket

MAP C5 ■ Montes da Luz, Praia da Luz ■ www.supermercado-baptista.com

Baptista is known for its fresh regional produce. On Saturdays there are occasional live cooking demonstrations, with tasting sessions later.

7 Sagres Natura Surf Shop

MAP B6 ■ Rua de São Vicente, Sagres

Come here for the wide range of top-brand surfwear, boards and accessories. The company also runs a well-established surf school, and rents kayaks and mountain bikes.

8 Aljezur Gypsy Market

MAP C3

A lively gypsy troupe trundles into Aljezur on the first Sunday of every month with an extraordinary array of clothing, household items and foodstuffs at bargain prices.

9 Mercado da Avenida

MAP D5 ■ Avenida dos Descobrimentos, Lagos ■ Open 8am–2pm Mon–Sat

A bustling fish market with a rooftop terrace restaurant and splendid views across the harbour.

10 Intermarché

MAP B6 ■ ER268, Sagres

On the main approach road to Sagres, this is the place at which to stock up on food, drink, toiletries and everyday essentials. Clothes, shoes, tools and kitchenware are also for sale. There is also an on-site café.

Places to Eat

PRICE CATEGORIES

For a three-course meal for one with half a bottle of wine (or equivalent meal), taxes and extra charges.

€ under €30 ■ €€ €30–€50 ■ €€€ over €50

① Cacto, Odiáxere
MAP D4 ■ EN 125, Odiáxere ■ (282) 798 285 ■ Closed Wed & Thu ■ D only ■ €€

Creamy pepper, garlic or blue-cheese sauce tops the tournedos "fillet" steak at this lively eatery.

Shaded terrace at Cacto, Odiáxere

② Adega Vila Lisa, Mexilhoeira Grande
MAP D4 ■ 52 Rua Francisco Bivar, Mexilhoeira Grande ■ (282) 968 478 ■ D only ■ Closed Oct–Jun: Sun–Thu No credit cards ■ No veg dishes ■ €€

A rural gem (see p70) with fine traditional cuisine, including succulent pork knee roast.

③ Mullen's, Lagos
MAP D5 ■ Rua Cândido Reis, 86, Lagos ■ (918) 480 071 ■ D only ■ Closed mid-Jan–Feb ■ €

This place is full of character and run by friendly staff. The Mozambique-style beef is incredible. Vegetarian food can be requested in advance.

④ O Terraço, Martinhal
MAP B6 ■ Hotel Martinhal, Martinhal ■ (282) 240 200 ■ D only ■ No veg dishes ■ €€€

A family-friendly restaurant, O Terraço (see p70) serves fresh regional food.

⑤ No Pátio, Lagos
MAP D5 ■ Rua Lançarote de Freitas 46, Lagos ■ (282) 763 777 ■ Closed Sun, Mon & last wk in Nov ■ €€

A charming alfresco restaurant that is popular with foodies.

⑥ Cabrita, Carrapateira
MAP B4 ■ 8670-230 Bordeira Carrapateira ■ (282) 973 128 ■ Closed Wed & Dec ■ No veg dishes ■ €

Located close to Praia do Amado (see p102), this eatery serves fresh fish and seafood in a friendly atmosphere.

⑦ Bica Boa, Monchique
MAP E3 ■ Estrada de Lisboa, 266, Monchique ■ (282) 912 271 ■ €

Sit on the terrace during fine weather for a wholesome alfresco treat.

⑧ Vila Velha, Sagres
MAP B6 ■ Rua Patrão António Faustino, Sagres ■ (282) 624 788 ■ Tue–Sun D ■ Closed Jan & Feb ■ €€

Oven-baked stuffed quail with Muscatel wine and raisin sauce is just one of the eclectic dishes here.

⑨ A Eira do Mel, Vila do Bispo
MAP B5 ■ Estrada do Castelejo, Vila do Bispo ■ (282) 639 016 ■ Closed Sun & Mon L ■ €€

This rural Slow Food member offers a superb Atlantic wild-shrimp cataplana and delicious desserts.

⑩ Mirandus, Lagos
MAP D5 ■ Romantik Hotel Vivenda Miranda, Porto de Mós, Lagos ■ (282) 763 222 ■ Closed Nov–Mar ■ €€

This gourmet restaurant serves fantastic food and offers breathtaking views of the ocean and the coastline.

See map on p98

𝗧𝗢𝗣𝟭𝟬 The Alentejo

Undulating plains and blistering summer heat characterize much of this province to the north of the Algarve. Neatly combed vineyards embroider along huge tracts of land, and much of the sun-baked earth is pocked by stubby cork and olive trees. Whitewashed villages are surrounded by emerald vines growing on ochre soil. To the north, medieval settlements perch on steep, granite escarpments in an altogether rockier terrain. Down by the coast, secluded beaches of golden sand brush sleepy, unhurried resorts that wake up in summer, when the days are long and the air is warm.

Remains of the Templo Romano in Évora

THE ALENTEJO

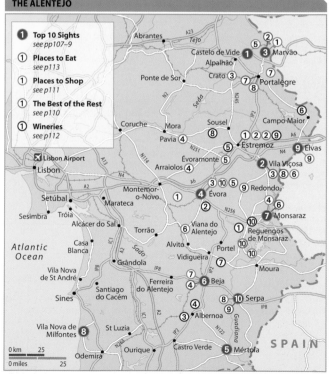

1 Top 10 Sights
see pp107–9

1 Places to Eat
see p113

1 Places to Shop
see p111

1 The Best of the Rest
see p110

1 Wineries
see p112

1 Castelo de Vide
Tourist info: Praça Dom Pedro V; (245) 908 227

The old Jewish quarter is the most enjoyable part of this attractive hilltop town. It stretches away from the 13th-century castle that gives the town its name in a cluster of steep lanes, many sporting plaques testifying to the quality of their floral displays. A synagogue (also 13th century) sits at the top of this stepped thoroughfare, which also leads down to the 16th-century marble Fonte da Vila.

2 Vila Viçosa
Tourist info: Praça da República; (268) 889 317

During the 15th century, Vila Viçosa became the country seat of the dukes of Bragança, and the town is best-known today for its splendid Paço Ducal. The sturdy battlements of the dukes' former abode, the castle, surround colourful cottages, two excellent museums and the 14th-century church of Nossa Senhora da Conceição.

3 Marvão
Tourist info: Rua da Silveirinha; (245) 909 131

Named "the eagle's nest" by locals, this medieval hamlet, set high upon on a rugged escarpment, is an astonishing sight. Sinuous 13th-century battlements envelop an immaculate village, where polished cobbled streets snake past neat façades, whitewashed cottages, a dainty church, trim gardens and a cherished museum. The castle has commanding views of the Serra de Marvão and the borderlands.

Fountain in Évora's Praça do Giraldo

4 Évora
Tourist info: Praça do Giraldo 73; (266) 777 071

The historic centre of the capital of the Alentejo is listed as a UNESCO World Heritage Site. Stunning examples of Roman, Moorish, medieval and 17th-century architecture abound in the old town *(see p109)*. The central Praça do Giraldo has a wonderful 16th-century fountain. A walk from the square up the lively Rua 5 de Outubro leads to the grandiose Sé (cathedral). An adjacent 16th-century palace houses the Museu de Évora. Adega Cartuxa offers visitors a classic Portuguese wine *(see p112)*.

Stunning views of the Castelo de Marvão

The historic town of Mértola

5 Mértola
Tourist info: Rua da Igreja 31; (286) 610 109

Designated a *vila museu*, or open-air museum town, the old quarter of Mértola is divided into a number of areas of historic interest. Each reflects diverse periods in the town's history: Phoenicians, Romans, Visigoths and Moors all took advantage of its strategic position on the River Guadiana. A number of museums exhibit treasures from each period, but the most stunning collection can be found in the Museu Islâmico.

6 Beja
Tourist info: inside the castle, Largo Dr Lima Faleiro; (284) 311 913

A thriving agricultural town and capital of the Baixo Alentejo, Beja

Nossa Senhora da Conceição in Beja

also has a rich past displayed in museum buildings that are often as interesting as their exhibits. The Convento de Nossa Senhora da Conceição, for example, now houses the Museu Regional, and the town's oldest church – the 6th-century Santo Amaro – is home to the Museu Visigótico. The landmark Torre de Menagem (castle keep) dates from the late 13th century.

7 Monsaraz
Tourist info: Rua Direita; (927) 997 316

Swathes of vineyards surround Monsaraz, a name synonymous with some of the finest Portuguese wines. The views from the granite walls of the 13th-century castle take in the huge man-made lake that has transformed the country-side. At dawn, the rising sun paints the water's surface a blaze of orange. The village's Igreja Matriz holds court over a maze of lanes lined with squat dwellings and restaurants.

8 Vila Nova de Milfontes
Tourist info: Rua António Mantas; (283) 996 599

This attractive town on the coast provides a welcome contrast from Alentejo's sun-parched interior. The old quarter is a hotchpotch of cobbled lanes and whitewashed cottages near a 16th-century sea fort, built to guard the town from pirates and buccaneers. The beaches – almost completely deserted out of season – are a popular summer attraction.

9 Elvas
Tourist info: Praça da República; (268) 622 236; www.fortegraca.aiaradc.org

Broad pentagonal bastions, star-shaped walls and gaping moats surround this busy frontier town near the Spanish border. The 17th-century military fortifications are among the finest in Europe and are listed as a UNESCO World Heritage Site. The battlements are best viewed from the late 15th-century castle. Elvas is also celebrated for the mighty Aqueduto da Amoreira and the outlying Forte de Santa Luzia and Forte da Graça.

Aqueduto da Amoreira in Elvas

10 Serpa
Tourist info: Rua dos Cavalos 19; (284) 544 727

This tranquil town is ideal for leisurely exploration. Start with the city walls and the stout towers of the Porta de Beja. Then discover the 17th-century aqueduct and noria. Within the walls, the castle provides the main focal point, and its ramparts offer sweeping views. Leave time to sample some *queijo Serpa* – a creamy ewe's milk cheese.

Porta de Beja in Serpa

A DAY IN ÉVORA

To Adega Cartuxa 2 km (1.2 miles), Rota dos Vinhos do Alentejo 500 m (550 yards) · Templo Romano · Museu de Évora · Sé · Café Arcada · Praça do Giraldo · Rua 5 de Outubro · Igreja de São Francisco

▶ MORNING

Begin at the Praça do Giraldo and wander up Rua 5 de Outubro towards the Sé (cathedral). Look out for the 14th-century carved Apostles flanking the portal and, once inside, climb to the treasury to see the 13th-century ivory figure of the Virgin.

Adjacent to the cathedral is the Museu de Évora, where a dazzling 16th-century Flemish polyptych, *Life of the Virgin*, can be found upstairs.

On the opposite side of the square are the granite Corinthian columns of the Templo Romano – the best-preserved Roman monument in Portugal.

From here, retrace your steps back to Praça do Giraldo for lunch or a coffee and queijada de Évora at Café Arcada *(Praça do Giraldo 7)*.

AFTERNOON

A few minutes' walk southeast from Praça do Giraldo is the impressive 16th-century Manueline-Gothic Igreja de São Francisco. The church's principal attraction is the eerie Capela dos Ossos (Bone Chapel), where the skeletal remains of some 5,000 monks line the walls and columns.

After this macabre experience, go back along Praça do Giraldo to Rota dos Vinhos do Alentejo for some wine-tasting. Alternatively, head outside the old town walls for the winery at **Adega Cartuxa** *(see p112)*. Arrive at 3pm or 4:30pm for a tour of this historic winery and the cellars.

See map on p106 ←

The Best of the Rest

1 Cromlech of Almendres, Guadalupe

The Cromlech of Almendres stone circles are considered to be the most important megalith group in the Iberian peninsula. Nearby is the Neolithic Dolmen of Zambujeiro.

Cromlech of Almendres

2 Estremoz

The handcrafted clay figures of Estremoz are a spectacular find, declared as the Intangible Cultural Heritage of Humanity by UNESCO.

3 Crato

The Mosteiro de Flor da Rosa was once the headquarters of the 14th-century Order of Hospitaliers and is now a historic *pousada*. Exhibits in the Museu Municipal (closed Mon and Tue) explain more about Crato's illustrious past.

4 Arraiolos and Pavia

Arraiolos is celebrated for its handmade rugs; the Interpretation Centre in Praça do Município houses a fine collection. In Pavia, 18 km (11 miles) to the north, a tiny chapel has been built into a dolmen – something unique in Portugal.

5 Évoramonte

Dramatic views reward those who make it to Évoramonte's castle walls, which are embellished with curious stone "ropes". Dom Miguel famously ceded the throne here on 26 May 1834.

6 Viana do Alentejo

A little backwater famed for its natural springs, but also home to a fine 14th-century castle and a fortified church. To enjoy the vibrant Romaria a Cavalo festivities, arrive here on the last weekend of April.

7 Serra de São Mamede

This beautiful and diverse nature park is home to a stunning variety of wildlife: Bonelli's eagle, blue rock thrush, genet and the Iberian midwife toad are just some of the park's residents.

8 Portalegre

The superb Museu Guy Fino (named in honour of the founder of Portalegre's only remaining tapestry factory) showcases some of the finest examples of contemporary tapestry in Europe.

9 Redondo

Dozens of hole-in-the-wall *olarias* (pottery workshops) line the streets of Redondo– a great place to buy ceramic souvenirs.

10 Barragem de Alqueva

Europe's biggest artificial reservoir. A marina at Amieira runs houseboat sightseeing holidays, and there is a fine traditional restaurant.

Pretty Arraiolos

Places to Shop

① Mercearia de Marvão, Marvão
Rua do Espírito Santo 1
A grocery, handicraft store and tavern all under the same roof, selling jams, cakes, honey, wines and liqueurs, as well as regional souvenirs crafted from local materials.

② Mercearia Gadanha, Estremoz
Largo Dragões de Olivença 84
Stock up at this traditional deli with goat's and ewe's milk cheeses, olives, hams and the town's famous preserved plums. There is also a selection of teas and wines. The on-site restaurant is open for lunch and dinner.

Ewe's milk cheese from Mercearia Gadanha

③ Divinus Gourmet, Évora
Mercado Municipal de Évora, Praça 1 de Maio
A mouth-watering selection of more than 500 gourmet goodies, including chocolates, jams, pâtés and wines.

④ Coisas de Monsaraz, Monsaraz
Largo do Castelo 2
Homemade jams and other assorted knick-knacks can be bought from this little arts and crafts shop nestling in the shadows of the castle walls.

⑤ Terrius
Edifício Moinha da Cova, Portagem ■ www.terrius.pt
Focusing on regional produce, this splendid cultural and environmental centre also offers cookery and cork handicraft workshops.

⑥ Mercado Municipal, Vila Viçosa
Largo D. João IV ■ 9am–1pm, daily
Housed in a modern complex in the town centre, Vila Viçosa's market is at its busiest early on Saturday mornings, when it overflows with fresh fruit and vegetables, and a wide selection of fish.

⑦ Portas de Mértola, Beja
This lively pedestrian zone is dotted with traditional shops and cafés, as well as places such as Maltesinhas and Café Luiz da Rocha.

⑧ Casa de Artesanato, Serpa
Rua dos Cavalos 33
A wonderfully atmospheric store packed full of hand-crafted goodies, including pots, shoes, handbags and blankets. The honey, cheeses, sausages and olive oil make lovely picnic ingredients.

⑨ Rua de Alcamim, Elvas
A busy, attractive pedestrianized street with florists, music stores, shoe shops and the usual handicrafts. The weekly Monday market takes place near the impressive Aqueduto da Amoreira.

⑩ Rua 5 de Outubro, Évora
Lined with *artesanatos* (craft shops) selling ceramics, carved cork, copper *cataplanas* (cooking pots), hand-painted chairs and other curios. On the second Tuesday of every month an open-air market takes place across the Rossio de São Brás, outside the town walls.

Ceramics stall, Évora

See map on p106

Wineries

The expansive Adega Mayor vineyards

1 Herdade do Esporão
Herdade do Esporão, Reguengos de Monsaraz ▪ (266) 509 280 ▪ Visits 11am, 3pm ▪ Advance booking required

Visit the vineyards, cellar and the Perdigões Archaeological Complex – a pre-historic monument.

2 Adega Cartuxa
Quinta de Valbom, Estrada da Soeira, Évora ▪ (266) 748 383 ▪ Visits 10:30am, 11:30am, 3pm & 4:30pm ▪ Advance booking required

This historic winery is home to the celebrated Pêra-Manca. The old cellars house a wine press from 1776.

3 Herdade da Malhadinha Nova
Albernôa, Alentejo ▪ (284) 965 210 ▪ Jun–Sep: Visits 11am, noon, 4pm & 5pm Mon–Sat; Oct–May: 11am, noon, 4pm & 5pm Mon–Sat ▪ Advance booking required

Apart from touring the vineyards and cellars, visitors are encouraged to study the wine labels, which are designed by the owners' children.

4 Herdade dos Grous
Albernôa, Alentejo ▪ (284) 960 000 ▪ Visits 11am & 4pm daily ▪ Advance booking required

A tour of the vineyard and winery is followed by tastings in the rustic bar.

5 João Portugal Ramos
Vila Santa, Estremoz ▪ (268) 339 910 ▪ Visits 9am–6:30pm Mon–Fri, 10am–6pm Sat (only for groups of 10 or more) ▪ Advance booking required

Tours, lunch and tasting sessions are offered at this respected winery.

6 Adega Mayor
Herdade das Argamassas, Campo Maior ▪ (268) 699 440 ▪ Visits 10am, 1pm, 3pm & 6pm daily ▪ Advance booking required

This winery has a tasting room with views across a lake and over to Spain.

7 Cortes de Cima
Vidigueira, Alentejo ▪ (284) 460 060 ▪ Visits 9am, noon, 1pm & 4pm ▪ Advance booking required

Guided tastings, accompanied by olive oil and bread, are held in a salon with views over the vineyards.

8 Herdade do Mouchão
Casa Branca Sousel, Portalegre Alentejo ▪ (268) 530 210 ▪ Open 8am–noon & 1–5pm Mon–Fri ▪ Advance booking required

This *adega* has produced wine and *aguardente* brandy since the late 19th century. Facilities are quite limited.

9 Dona Maria
Quinta do Carmo, Estremoz ▪ (268) 339 150 ▪ Visits 10am & 5pm Sat ▪ Advance booking required

This is a picturesque winery with an 18th-century chapel and gardens.

10 Adega José de Sousa
Rua de Mourão 1, Reguengos de Monsaraz, Alentejo ▪ (266) 502 729 ▪ Visits Apr–Oct: 10am, noon, 2:30pm & 5:30pm Mon–Sat; Nov–Mar: 10am, noon, 2:30pm & 4:30pm ▪ Advance booking required

Famed for its astonishing clay amphorae cellar with a Romanesque ceiling, this is one of the world's most unusual wine cellars.

Streetsmart

Traditional ceramics from Sagres

Places to Eat

1 Gadanha Mercearia
**Largo Dragões de Olivença 84a,
Estremoz ▪ (268) 333 262 ▪ Closed
Mon ▪ No vegetarian dishes ▪ €**
This rustic eatery combines
a restaurant and a wine shop,
and also features a grocery store
packed with regional goodies.

2 Restaurante Casa do Povo
**Travessa do Chabouco, Marvão
▪ (245) 993 160 ▪ Closed Thu
▪ No vegetarian dishes ▪ €**
Sweeping terrace views and hearty
portions of regional food in one of
Portugal's most beautiful mountain
villages makes dining here a treat.

Interior of Pousada Vila Viçosa

3 Pousada Vila Viçosa – D. João IV
**Terreiro do Paço, Vila Viçosa
▪ (268) 980 742 ▪ €€**
Be sure to opt for the regional menu
at this beautiful former convent –
dishes are based on the recipes
of the nuns who used to live here.

4 A Pipa
**Rua da Moeda 8, Beja ▪ (284)
327 043 ▪ Open noon–2:30pm &
7:30–10:30pm Mon–Sat ▪ €**
Grilled pork is a signature dish at
this delightfully rustic restaurant.

5 Fialho
**Travessa dos Mascarenhas 16,
Évora ▪ (266) 703 079 ▪ Closed Mon,
Jun & Jul ▪ No vegetarian dishes ▪ €€**
Local specialities include *cacão de
coentrada* (dog fish with coriander
sauce). Advance booking is essential.

6 Xarez
**Rua de Santiago 33, Monsaraz
▪ (266) 557 052 ▪ Closed Jan,
Wed D, Thu; D only in summer
▪ No vegetarian dishes ▪ €**
A menu of regional fare is served
at this chic restaurant. It offers
breathtaking views from the terrace.

7 Na Boca do Lobo
**Ave Alexandre Herculano
20, Portalegre ▪ (965) 416 630
▪ Closed Sun & Mon ▪ €**
Prepared by chef José Júlio, among
the vast options of local fare, the
menu includes *pernas da rã* (frog
legs), a mouth-watering surprise.

8 Os Cucos
**Mata Municipal, Vila Viçosa
▪ (268) 980 806 ▪ Closed 1–15 Aug
▪ No vegetarian dishes ▪ €**
Set in verdant, shady gardens, this
eatery offers a daily menu, usually
featuring earthy Alentejan fare.
There is also an outside terrace.

9 Restaurante Alentejano
**Praça da República, Serpa
▪ (284) 544 335 ▪ Closed Sun pm,
Mon & Jul ▪ No vegetarian dishes ▪ €**
Order the *ensopado de borrego
a pastora* (lamb stew, shepherd-
ess style) for a real taste of
the Alentejo.

10 Restaurante Panorâmico da Amieira
**Amieira Marina, Amieira ▪ (266) 611
175 ▪ Apr–Oct: L Thu–Tue, D Fri–Sun;
Nov–Mar: L Fri–Mon, D Fri–Sun
▪ No vegetarian dishes ▪ €**
Try to sit at a terrace table at this
restaurant for views of the lake.
Delicious Alentejo cuisine.

See map on p106

Getting To and Around the Algarve

Arriving by Air

The entry/exit point for visitors by plane is **Faro International Airport**, located 6 km (4 miles) west of the city centre. The airport serves both domestic and foreign carriers from all over Europe. Flights from the US and other transatlantic destinations route through Lisbon. Canadian carrier **Air Transat**, however, operates a direct Toronto–Faro service late Jan to mid-April. The national airline, **TAP Portugal**, operates daily scheduled services between Faro and Lisbon and Oporto.

The airport website lists daily arrivals and departures. There are good public transport links into town from the terminal. Local buses 14 and 16 run daily to the centre, departing every half an hour from 5am until 11pm. A taxi from the airport into the town centre should cost around €12–14.

Arriving by Rail

Faro Railway Station is located on Largo da Estação, near the harbour. **Comboios de Portugal** (CP) operates all trains: the daily high-speed Alfa Pendular (AP) and intercity services (IC) from Lisbon, Oporto and Braga terminate here.

Passengers can choose to travel *conforto* (first-class) or *turística* (second-class). Seat reservations are obligatory, although they are included in the ticket price. Faro is also on the Algarve rail line, which runs from Lagos in the west to Vila Real de Santo António on the Spanish border.

Arriving by Road

A tolled motorway (A2) links Lisbon with the Algarve. Tickets are issued from toll booths when you join a motorway and redeemed at the next booth, or when you leave. The cost depends on the distance travelled and vehicle class. Do not use the Via Verde lane at tolls; this is only for drivers who subscribe to an electronic pre-payment system.

Unless you exit at São Bartolomeu de Messines (junction 14), continuing on the A2 south will bring you onto the A22 motorway (Via do Infante). Be aware that this is an electronically tolled highway that uses number-plate-recognition cameras to charge. If you are driving your own vehicle you have three different ways of paying. The **Portugal Tolls** website details the methods. If using a hire car you need to pay for road usage at a post office: quote your registration number to find out how much you owe. Some rental-car companies have fitted their fleets with transponders, which automatically record travel on the A22. Upon return of the vehicle, your credit card will be charged the applicable fee. A website, **Car Hire Faro Airport**, provides more information on this.

An alternative way to drive to the Algarve is to use the IC1. Though slower, the road is more scenic and avoids the tolled A2. The A49 from Huelva in Spain crosses the bridge over the Rio Guadiana to merge with the A22 near the town of Vila Real de Santo António.

Arriving by Coach

There are excellent express coach services to the Algarve from cities across Portugal. The three main companies are **EVA Transportes**, **Renex** and **Rede Expressos**. Tickets can be purchased on the day of travel from bus stations and ticket desks, but it is prudent to book ahead, especially during the busy summer months.

Travelling by Train

The regional railway line connects Vila Real de Santo António on the Spanish border with Lagos. While slow, the service is inexpensive and you can purchase a ticket onboard. If you plan to use the train regularly consider buying a discounted 2-day (€20.90) or 3-day (€31.90) Tourist Travel Card, which are available at larger train stations.

Travelling by Bus

All the major coach companies, including **Frota Azul**, operate fast and efficient regional services between major coastal and inland towns. However, some rural bus travel is slow and schedules are sometimes unpredictable. Always put your arm out to flag down an approaching bus. Note that, confusingly, bus stop signs *(paragem)* can be on the opposite side of the road, against the direction of intended travel.

Travelling by Car

A car allows you more freedom to explore the region. Driving is on the right. The speed limit is 50 km/h (35 mph) in towns and villages, 90 km/h (60 mph) on normal roads and 120 km/h (80 mph) on motorways. Safety belts (front and back) are compulsory.

Drivers must carry a red warning triangle and a fluorescent yellow jacket in case of an accident or breakdown. If you are stopped by the police, your personal ID or passport, driving licence and insurance policy will be requested. Proof of ownership will also be needed if it is your own vehicle.

Hiring a car is a popular option. The minimum age for rental is 21. Several international car-hire companies have offices at Faro airport. Rental agencies, including local firms such as **Auto Jardim**, can be found in the major towns and seaside resorts.

Travelling by Taxi

A relatively inexpensive travel option, taxis are widely used in the Algarve.

The starting rate for a taxi hailed in the street or flagged at a rank is €3.25. If you phone for a cab an extra 80 cents is levied. Additional charges will be made for carrying luggage, and rates increase by 25 per cent from 9pm to 6am, at weekends and on public holidays. Charges are posted inside the taxi. Note that it is not always cost-effective to travel short distances, because tariffs are usually fixed. Outside towns, journeys by taxi are per kilometre, so establish a price beforehand. Tipping is discretionary, though 5–10 per cent of the total fare is fair. The **Aeroporto de Faro** website has a taxi-service operation page.

Tickets

Tickets for AP and IC trains can usually be booked up to 30 days ahead, and considerable discounts can be enjoyed on advance purchase (at least five days) and return tickets. There are also additional 50 per cent discounts for children aged 5–12 (under-5s go free) and for passengers aged 65 and over. Students with valid youth cards also receive discounts.

If a regional rail station is unstaffed you can pay the ticket inspector on board for your ticket. To benefit from any travel discounts you will need to show proof of identity. You can either book long-distance tickets online or buy them at bus stations, but they cannot be purchased directly from the driver.

Increasingly, digital tickets are being issued to mobile devices. **EVA Transportes** has a 3-day (€30.10) and a 7-day (€37.50) Tourist Pass for unlimited travel in the Algarve on its extensive bus network.

DIRECTORY

ARRIVING BY AIR
Air Transat
w airtransat.com

Faro International Airport
MAP K6 ▪ 8001-701 Faro
📞 (289) 800 800
w ana.pt

TAP Portugal
w flytap.com

ARRIVING BY RAIL
Comboios de Portugal
w cp.pt

Faro Railway Station
MAP K6 ▪ Largo de Estação, Faro
📞 (707) 210 220

ARRIVING BY ROAD
Car Hire Faro Airport
w carhirefaroairport.com

Portugal Tolls
w portugaltolls.pt

ARRIVING BY COACH
EVA Transportes
w eva-bus.com

Rede Expressos
w rede-expressos.pt

Renex
w renex.com

TRAVELLING BY BUS
Frota Azul
w frotazul-algarve.pt

TRAVELLING BY CAR
Auto Jardim
w auto-jardim.com

TRAVELLING BY TAXI
Aeroporto de Faro
w en.aeroportodefaro.com/taxis

Practical Information

Passports and Visas

Residents of the European Economic Area (EEA) and European Union (EU), and Swiss nationals need only a valid passport or identity card to enter Portugal. If they stay for longer than 6 months they should apply for a residence permit. Citizens of Canada, the **US**, **Australia** and **New Zealand** can visit Portugal for up to 90 days without a visa as long as their passport is valid for 6 months beyond the date of entry. Most other non-EU and non-EEA nationals (including South Africans) need a visa, and should consult a Portuguese embassy or consulate before departure. Once you are in the country, the Foreigner's Registration Service, **Serviço de Estrangeiros e Fronteiras**, can arrange a visa extension if necessary – it has offices in the Algarve.

Customs and Immigration

For EU citizens there are no limits on most goods carried in or out of Portugal as long as they are for personal use. Exceptions include firearms, weapons, some types of food and plants, and protected and endangered species. Non-EU citizens can import 200 cigarettes and a litre of spirits per adult, and can claim back the sales tax (IVA) on purchases that cost more than €61.35 – this can be done at the airport when leaving the EU.

Travel Safety Advice

Visitors can get up-to-date safety information from the **UK Foreign and Commonwealth Office**, the **US Department of State** and the **Australian Department of Foreign Affairs and Trade**.

Travel Insurance

All travellers are advised to take out comprehensive travel insurance to cover against illness or injury and loss, theft and delays or cancellations. Note that most watersports activities are not covered by policies unless an extra premium is paid. The European Health Insurance Card (EHIC) allows EU citizens access to Portugal's public healthcare system under reciprocal agreements. In the event of minor injuries or illness, you will need to produce a valid card together with your passport at a health centre or hospital for free or reduced-cost medical treatment. Prescriptions have to be paid for upfront.

Health

The Algarve has three hospitals: in Faro, Lagos and Portimão. **Hospital de Faro** is the largest facility and offers *urgência* (emergency) services. Most doctors speak English. If you require medical assistance for minor injuries, you should go to the local *centro da saúde* (health centre).

No vaccinations are required in order to enter Portugal, though it is a good idea to be up-to-date with flu and tetanus jabs. *Farmácias* (pharmacies) are easily identifiable by their green cross sign, and are found everywhere. Out of hours, the address of the nearest late-closing (10pm) or all-night pharmacy is posted. **SmartExpat** provides useful information regarding healthcare for visitors in Portugal.

Personal Security

The Algarve enjoys a reputation as a safe and peaceful destination. Violent crime is very rare. However, petty theft is a problem in the holiday resorts during the crowded summer months. Taking a few sensible precautions, such as not flaunting expensive items will lessen the risk of being targeted by pickpockets and bag-snatchers. Never leave valuables or cash unattended, and make use of hotel in-room safes, if available.

The **Associação Portuguesa de Apoio à Vítima** (APAV) is a support group that helps victims of crime, including tourists. A dedicated unit, **Police Support Services for Tourists**, operates in the Algarve where visitors can report assaults, thefts and lost property.

Women travelling alone in the Algarve are quite safe, although common safety principles, such as keeping to well-lit, public places after dark, should be adhered to. It is best to avoid remote inland areas.

Emergency Services

The number to dial in an **emergency** is 112. The call can be answered in three different languages: Portuguese, English and French. Ask for the service you require – *polícia* (police), *ambulância* (ambulance) or *bombeiros* (fire brigade). In the event of an accident on the motorway, and with no access or signal to a mobile phone, look for one of the orange SOS telephone kiosks sited intermittently along the hard shoulder. The service is available in Portuguese only. Press the button and then wait for the operator who will connect you.

Travellers with Specific Needs

MyWay is a personalized support service for air passengers with limited mobility, travelling in a EU member state. The service must be pre-booked with the air carrier when reserving the flight. Passengers are assisted with luggage and are escorted to and from their aircraft seat. At Faro International Airport, look for the designated MyWay service points.

Many of the Algarve's four- and five-star hotels have at least one room specifically designed to accommodate guests with mobility issues.

Accessible Portugal is a Lisbon-based travel agency with English-speaking staff. Specializing in arranging holidays for those with special needs, it also arranges transfers by vehicles adapted for carrying wheelchairs.

Faro-based **Algarve Accessible** lists wheelchair-friendly accommodation and attractions, and offers mobility aids for hire.

DIRECTORY

PASSPORTS AND VISAS

Australia
Embassy, Av da Liberdade 200, 2 Piso, Lisbon
📞 (213) 101 500
🌐 portugal.embassy. gov.au

New Zealand
Honorary Consul,
Rua da Sociedade Farmacêutica 68,
1 Dto, Lisbon
📞 (213) 140 780
🌐 mfat.govt.nz

Serviço de Estrangeiros e Fronteiras
🌐 sef.pt

UK
MAP E4
■ Honorary Consul,
Edf. A Fábrica, Av Guanaré, Portimão
📞 (282) 490 750
🌐 ukinportugal.fco. gov.uk

US
Embassy
Av das Forças Armadas, Lisbon
📞 (217) 273 300
🌐 pt.usembassy.gov

TRAVEL SAFETY ADVICE

Australian Department of Foreign Affairs and Trade
🌐 dfat.gov.au
🌐 smartraveller.gov.au

UK Foreign and Commonwealth Office
🌐 gov.uk/foreign-travel-advice

US Department of State
🌐 travel.state.gov

HEALTH

Hospital de Faro
MAP K6
■ Rua Leão Penedo
📞 (289) 891 100
🌐 hdfaro.min-saude.pt

Lagos Hospital
MAP D5
■ Rua Castelo dos Governadores
📞 (282) 770 100

Portimão Hospital
MAP E4
■ Sítio do Poço Seco
📞 (282) 450 300

SmartExpat
🌐 smartexpat.com

PERSONAL SECURITY

Associação Portuguesa de Apoio à Vítima
📞 (213) 587 914
🌐 apav.pt

Police Support Services For Tourists
Albufeira Police
📞 (289) 513 203
Tourist Help Line
📞 (808) 781 212
Vilamoura Police
📞 (289) 381 780

EMERGENCY SERVICES

Police, Ambulance and Fire Brigade
📞 112

TRAVELLERS WITH SPECIFIC NEEDS

Accessible Portugal
📞 (926) 910 989
🌐 accessibleportugal.com

Algarve Accessible
📞 (289) 810 100
🌐 algarve-accessible.com

MyWay
📞 (289) 800 800
🌐 flytap.com/en-pt/special-needs/my-way

Currency and Banking

Portugal uses the euro (€), the common currency of the European Union. One euro is divided into 100 cents. Paper notes are in denominations of €5, €10, €20, €50, €100, €200 and €500. Coins are €2, €1, 50c, 20c, 5c, 2c and 1c. Larger denomination banknotes, such as the €200 and €500 notes, have a limited circulation in Portugal, and some establishments may refuse to accept them.

Portugal has a national network of cash machines (ATMs) identifiable by the symbol MB, or Multibanco, from which you can withdraw cash 24 hours a day. While you will not be charged commission, bank surcharges still apply and it is best to enquire about credit-card ATM cash withdrawal fees before departure. Money can be changed at banks, bureaux de change *(agências de câmbios)* and at many larger hotels. There are bank branches everywhere and they tend to offer better exchange and commission rates.

The popular coastal resorts have financial service companies, such as Western Union, that can arrange person-to-person transfers.

Pre-paid currency cards (cash passports) are a more secure way of carrying money. They can be preloaded with euros (fixing exchange rates before you leave) and used like a credit card.

Mastercard and **Visa** credit and debit cards are widely accepted at shops and restaurants in the main towns and resorts, but there may be a minimum charge, generally €5–€10. **American Express** and other cards are less widely accepted. It is always wise to carry some cash, especially in rural areas.

Telephone and Internet

Many of the region's hotels, hostels and guesthouses offer Wi-Fi as a complimentary service, and provide guests with a password at check-in. Internet access is also available in many bars, cafés, restaurants, larger shopping malls and other public "hot spots", though sometimes you will need to register and pay for usage, typically €2 per hour (often free for Wi-Fi). Connections can be slower away from built-up areas.

To use your mobile phone in Portugal, it will need to be equipped for GSM network frequencies 900 and 1800 MHz. To avoid running up exorbitant roaming fees, consider purchasing a local SIM card or a cheap mobile phone so you can take advantage of local rates. Check with your home carrier whether you need to unlock your device to use a different SIM card/service. The international dialling code for Portugal is 351. Most public telephone booths now only accept a telephone card *(cartão telefónico)* available from post offices, newsagents and kiosks. Avoid making calls using a hotel telephone: charges are always high.

Postal Services

The postal service in Portugal is known as the **CTT Correios de Portugal**. Post offices *(correios)* are usually open weekdays 9am–6pm, with an hour for lunch. Some larger branches are open on Saturday mornings.

First-class mail is known as *correio azul* and second-class mail is called *normal*. *Correio azul* is posted in blue postboxes and everything else goes in red postboxes. Oversized items are taken over the counter. At some post offices there may also be separate slots for national and international post.

Stamps can be bought from post offices or from any shop which displays the red and white Correios sign. For express mail and parcels, using an international courier, such as **DHL**, may be a better option.

Television and Radio

Portugal's four domestic channels – RTP1, RTP2, SIC and TVI – are complemented by a bewildering array of other private, European and international television stations, aired by subscription-based cable or satellite channels. All foreign-language films, shows and series (except for animation) are shown in their original language, with Portuguese subtitles. National and local radio stations are numerous and, between news and sport bulletins, fairly mainstream in musical output. The Algarve has its very own English-language radio station,

Kiss FM (95.8 and 101.2 FM), which mixes music with news, weather reports and flight and travel bulletins.

Newspapers and Magazines

English-language newspapers printed in Europe are readily available at newsagents in larger towns and coastal resorts on the day of publication, including the *International New York Times*. Several other European newspapers and periodicals are also generally on sale the same day of home publication. The English-language *Portugal News* is a widely distributed weekly newspaper that includes Algarve domestic news. Similarly, the popular weekly *Algarve Resident* reports on national and international news, as well as issues affecting the region specifically. Portuguese daily newspapers include *Diário de Notícias* and *Público*. The heavyweight *Expresso* is Portugal's leading weekly newspaper.

Opening Hours

Generally, shop hours are 9am–1pm and 3–7pm, Mon–Fri. Most are also open all day Saturday from 9am–7pm in high season. Hours are often extended in coastal resorts during the high season, and Sunday trading is commonplace. Larger shopping centres and malls are open seven days a week until midnight. Normal banking hours are 8:30am–3pm, Mon–Fri. Some larger

branches in the Algarve are also open in the evenings during the summer months. Likewise, bureaux de change and financial services companies usually operate flexible hours to take advantage of the seasonal influx of tourists.

Museums, monuments, galleries and some churches tend to regulate their own visiting times, but are nearly always closed on Mondays as well as on Christmas Day, New Year's Day, and during Easter and other public holidays. As a rule, though, historic visitor attractions are open 10am–5pm Tue–Sun, with many establishments closing for lunch either at noon–2pm or at 12:30–2:30pm.

Time Difference

Portugal and Madeira operate on Western European Time, which is the same as Greenwich Mean Time (GMT) and is 5 hours ahead of US Eastern Standard Time (EST). The clock moves forward 1 hour during daylight saving time, which is from the last Sunday in March until the last Sunday in October.

Electrical Appliances

Portugal uses plugs with two round pins and an electrical mains voltage of 220V. Most hotel bathrooms offer built-in adaptors for electric appliances. Mobile adaptors can be purchased at Faro Airport and from electrical retail outlets.

Weather

Average daytime temperatures in summer hover between 24°C (75°F) and 29°C (84°F). In winter it rarely drops below 15°C (60°F), though inland it can become chilly. Spring and autumn are the best times to visit, avoiding the crowds in the hottest months of July and August.

DIRECTORY

CURRENCY AND BANKING

American Express
☎ (214) 270 400

Mastercard
☎ (800) 811 272

Visa
☎ (800) 811 107

POSTAL SERVICES

CTT Correios de Portugal
🌐 ctt.pt

DHL
🌐 dhl.pt

TELEVISION AND RADIO

Kiss FM
🌐 kissfm.pt

NEWSPAPERS AND MAGAZINES

Algarve Resident
🌐 portugalresident.com

Diário de Notícias
🌐 dn.pt/

Expresso
🌐 expresso.sapo.pt

International New York Times
🌐 nytimes.com

The Portugal News
🌐 theportugalnews.com

Público
🌐 publico.pt

Visitor Information

The **Visit Portugal** website offers a general overview of the region, though the **Turismo do Algarve** site provides more detailed information. Users can download various guides and an app for Android and iOS devices. They can also interact with fellow tourists on the *turismo de Portugal* Facebook page.

Other useful apps and websites for visitors include **TripAdvisor**, for reviews of hotels, restaurants and sights, and **Google Maps**, useful when planning itineraries. **Inspirations Algarve** features hotel and restaurant reviews and suggestions for leisure activities. **In Portugal** by Julie Fox explores the Algarve, in addition to other regions in Portugal, from a long-term resident's point of view. Another blog, **Algarve Experiences**, highlights the Algarve's culture and cuisine.

There is a tourist office in every major town across the region. Here you will find maps, brochures, pamphlets, accommodation tips and the tourist board's free monthly *Algarve Guide*. Hotel receptions are a good source of visitor information, and guests can often enjoy discounts if they book an attraction via staff at the front desk.

The region's beaches are some of the best in Europe. Beachgoers should note that a red flag hoisted over the sand indicates a strong tide or dangerous undertow, and swimming is prohibited. A yellow flag signifies caution – you should stay within your depth. When a green flag is flying, the water is safe.

Trips and Tours

City Sightseeing operates hop-on hop-off, open-top bus tours in and around Albufeira. The buses stop at all the main sights, including the beach. Fun-packed jeep safaris are organized by **Algarve Jeep Safari**, and travel well off the beaten track. The more adventurous can take the wheel in one of their custom-made buggies.

Algarve Online arranges tours and excursions by private coach to all areas of the region, plus extended journeys to other parts of Portugal and southern Spain.

Formosamar arranges activities that are certified as Ecotourism by the Portuguese Institute for Conservation of Nature and Biodiversity. The company promotes the natural and cultural heritage of the Ria Formosa area.

Renting a Segway from **Algarve by Segway** provides a novel way of sightseeing. Tour options include a trip to the peak of Fóia *(see p20)*.

The Mountain Bike Adventure has qualified guides that lead expeditions over some of Europe's finest tracks.

One of the quirkiest ways to roam the region is by motorized rickshaw. **Love Tuk Olhão** combines city tours with excursions to the nearby Parque Natural da Ria Formosa *(see pp30–33)*.

Nature enthusiasts, meanwhile, can enjoy a boat trip with **Natura Algarve** and sail alongside dolphins. The River Guadiana is the backdrop for trips organized by **Fun River**. The company also arranges designed heritage-themed walks and bicycle rides.

Shopping

One of the joys of visiting the Algarve is to discover the region's bustling markets. Two of the largest are at Loulé and Olhão *(see pp74–5)*. Shoppers should always check for any restrictions on importing foodstuffs into their home country.

Traditional handicrafts make ideal souvenirs, and at Casa dos Arcos you can buy wooden *cadeiras de tesoura (see p104)*. Ceramics and earthenware also make wonderful gifts. Cork products are original and eco-friendly, and **Pelcor** sells an amazing range of handbags, wallets and fashion accessories, manufactured entirely from cork skin.

Supermarket chain **Apolónia** *(see p75)* is known for its delicatessen counter and excellent choice of wine, and has several stores located across the region.

Dining

The Algarve can claim a unique cooking utensil, the *cataplana*. Made from copper and consisting of two close-fitting concave halves, resembling a wok with handles that snap together, this unusual vessel is essentially a steaming device used to cook dishes such as *amêijoas na cataplana* – cockles with white wine, garlic and herbs. Fish and seafood are very prominent on restaurant menus: the ubiquitous sardine is a summer staple, charcoal-grilled and best eaten using your fingers.

High season in the Algarve sees many restaurants extend their opening hours beyond midnight. Restaurant choice is vast, with a wide range of tastes catered for.

The Algarve has the greatest concentration of Michelin-starred restaurants anywhere in Portugal, and many other top-range establishments are "recommended" in the coveted Red Guide.

There are also plenty of humble eateries where simple, tasty fare is served. Many offer an inexpensive *prato do dia* (dish of the day). Children's menus are commonplace, and weekends and public holidays will see local families dining out en masse.

Some establishments insist on advance bookings, and this is wise during the busy summer months. **Dining Out** lists a good cross-section of region-wide restaurants, although vegetarian options are rare.

Accommodation

There is an outstanding range of accommodation in the Algarve, from luxury resort hotels to hostels, self-catering apartments and farmhouses. There are also restored palaces and sea forts to consider, golf and country clubs, boutique boltholes and excellent campsites. Prices vary, depending on the season. Room rates are obviously higher during the summer months and at peak travel periods such as Easter, and often on Friday and Saturday nights. Prices plummet considerably during the winter.

Booking directly with the hotel online is usually the best way to arrange your stay, and many upmarket hotel websites feature offers and promotions to guests who do so. You can also compare prices on sites such as **Booking.com** and **Trivago**. Good, budget options include staying in a one-star hotel, classified as a *pensão* or *residencial*. These offer clean, value-for-money facilities and may provide meals or offer breakfast. You can also rent a room in a private house, known as a *quarto* – look out for signs in windows, or check with the local tourist office.

Pousadas de Juventude operates several youth hostels in the region. **Pousadas de Portugal** has three hotels in the Algarve. These are beautiful and historic properties offering luxury accommodation.

DIRECTORY

VISITOR INFORMATION

Algarve Experiences
🔲 algarveexperiences.com

Google Maps
🔲 maps.google.pt

In Portugal
🔲 juliedawnfox.com

Inspirations Algarve
🔲 inspirationsalgarve.com

TripAdvisor
🔲 tripadvisor.com

Turismo do Algarve
🔲 visitalgarve.pt

Visit Portugal
🔲 visitportugal.com

TRIPS AND TOURS

Algarve Jeep Safari
🔲 algarvejeepsafari.com

Algarve Online
🔲 algarve-tours-excursions.com

Algarve by Segway
🔲 algarvebysegway.com

City Sightseeing
🔲 city-sightseeing.com

Formosamar
🔲 formosamar.com

Fun River
🔲 fun-river.com

Love Tuk Olhão
🔲 lovetukolhao.pt

The Mountain Bike Adventure
🔲 themountainbikeadventure.com

Natura Algarve
🔲 natura-algarve.com

SHOPPING

Apolónia
🔲 apolonia.com

Pelcor
🔲 pelcor.pt

DINING

Dining Out
🔲 diningout.com.pt

ACCOMMODATION

Booking.com
🔲 booking.com

Pousadas de Juventude
🔲 pousadasjuventude.pt

Pousadas de Portugal
🔲 pestana.com

Trivago
🔲 trivago.com

Places to Stay

PRICE CATEGORIES

For a standard, double room per night (with breakfast if included), taxes and extra charges.

€ under €100   €€ €100–300   €€€ over €300

Luxury, Five-Star Hotels

Anantara Vilamoura Algarve Resort

MAP H5 ▪ Avenida dos Descobrimentos, Vilamoura ▪ (289) 317 000 ▪ www.vilamoura. anantara.pt ▪ €€

Overlooking the Oceânico Victoria golf course (see p60), this modern and attractive property boasts three pools and a tennis court among its premium guest facilities. The therapists at the Elements Spa by Banyan Tree deliver an authentic Oriental spa experience. Among the massages available is the Balinese massage, which stimulates circulation, increases energy flow and alleviates tension.

Cascade Wellness & Lifestyle Resort

MAP D5 ▪ Praia do Canavial, Lagos ▪ (282) 771 500 ▪ www.cascade resortalgarve.com ▪ €€€

Located on a secluded clifftop, all rooms and suites enjoy either pool or ocean views. Amenities include a spa, a golf academy, tennis courts and the Senses restaurant.

Conrad Algarve

MAP J5 ▪ Estrada do Quinta do Largo, Quinta do Largo ▪ (289) 350 700 ▪ www.conradalgarve. com ▪ €€€

Top-notch contemporary design and use of the latest technology define this exceptional property. Amenities include the Michelin-starred restaurant Gusto (see p89),, a spa, indoor and outdoor swimming pools, a children's club and nearby championship golf courses.

Hotel Quinta do Lago

MAP J5 ▪ Quinta do Lago, near Almancil ▪ (289) 350 350 ▪ www.hotelquintado lago.com ▪ €€€

Overlooking Ria Formosa lagoon and the ocean, this sophisticated resort has two excellent restaurants: the Brisa do Mar (traditional Portuguese cuisine) and Cá d'Oro (famed for its Italian gastronomy). Leisure facilities include a golf course and a health club with a gym and sauna.

Vila Joya Boutique Resort

MAP G5 ▪ Praia da Galé, Albufeira ▪ (289) 591 795 ▪ www.vilajoya.com ▪ €€€

An exclusive gourmet retreat, with splendid seafront gardens and a two-starred Michelin restaurant (see p71). Spa facilities and Ayurvedic massage are available.

Vila Vita Parc Resort & Spa

MAP F5 ▪ Alporchinhos, Porches, Armação de Pêra ▪ (282) 310 100 ▪ www. vilavitaparc.com ▪ €€€

At this luxury clifftop resort set above a secluded beach, Moorish-inspired architecture is complemented by contemporary flourishes. Guest amenities include the Vital Spa, an 18-hole putting green and a kids' park. The Ocean Restaurant has two Michelin stars (see p71).

Spa Hotels and Resorts

Hilton Vilamoura As Cascatas Golf Resort & Spa

MAP H5 ▪ Rua da Torre d'Agua, Vilamoura ▪ (289) 304 000 ▪ www. hiltonvilamouraresort. com.pt ▪ €€

Portugal's largest spa, 7 Seven Spa, is located here. Hydro-massage pools, ice fountains and aromatic steam baths exemplify the resort's aquatic theme. The invigorating water tunnel experience is a favourite option for guests. Treatments include a detox bath and a body wrap with sculpting massage.

Real Marina Hotel & Spa

MAP L5 ▪ Avenida 5 de Outubro, Olhão ▪ (289) 091 300 ▪ www. realmarina. realhotels group.com ▪ €€

The hydrotherapy treatments at the Real Spa Therapy are highly regarded and are offered as baths, wraps and massages. There are nine treatment rooms, and facilities include a Turkish bath, a sauna and a Vichy shower. The spa has wonderful views over the Ria Formosa.

Bela Vista Hotel & Spa
MAP E5 ▪ Avenida Tomás Cabreira, Praia da Rocha ▪ (282) 460 280 ▪ www. hotelbelavista.net ▪ €€€
Branded by L'Occitane, the boutique spa uses some of the region's traditions in its massage techniques: the "Ritual de Amêndoa Algarvia", for example, includes an exfoliation using almond paste. It also houses the Michelin-starred Vista Restaurant.

Epic Sana Algarve
MAP G5 ▪ Olhos de Água, Albufeira ▪ (289) 104 300 ▪ www.algarve.epic. sanahotels.com ▪ €€€
Guests can have massages and treatments in a garden pavilion at this modern oceanfront resort. The Sayanna Wellness experience also embraces an intoxicating variety of treatments designed by Aromatherapy Associates. Fitness retreats and boot camps can be arranged.

Pine Cliffs Resort
MAP G5 ▪ Praia da Falésia, Albufeira ▪ (289) 500 300 ▪ www.pinecliffs.com ▪ €€€
At 1000 sq m (3,300 sq ft), the Destination SPA serves the entire resort, including the Pine Cliffs Ocean Suites. The state-of-the-art facility, one of the newest in the Algarve, encompasses 11 treatment rooms and the impressive Spa Suite.

Vilalara Thalassa Resort
MAP F5 ▪ Praia das Gaivotas, Lagoa ▪ (282) 320 000 ▪ www. vilalara resort.com ▪ €€€€
Vilalara features one of the world's finest thalassotherapy (sea-water bathing) centres, as well as an extensive range of facilities and treatments for health, beauty and wellbeing. Two excellent restaurants on-site.

Resort Hotels for Families

Grande Real Santa Eulália Resort & Hotel Spa
MAP G5 ▪ Praia de Santa Eulália, Albufeira ▪ (289) 598 000 ▪ www.grande realsantaeulaliahotel.com ▪ €€
This five-star resort has direct beach access and offers pampering at its Real Spa Thalasso. Baby-sitting is offered with advance notice, and children can try activities at the complimentary children's club.

Hotel Algarve Casino
MAP E5 ▪ Avenida Tomás Cabreira, Praia da Rocha ▪ (282) 402 000 ▪ www. hotelalgarvecasino.com ▪ €€
This offers the complete family holiday package. Apart from the famous Praia da Rocha beach, leisure facilities on hand include a swimming pool, a video room, a children's zone and a casino that stages cabaret.

Hotel Belavista da Luz
MAP C5 ▪ Praia da Luz, Lagos ▪ (282) 788 655 ▪ www.belavistadaluz. com ▪ €€
A family-run hotel, built in a horseshoe shape to enclose two inviting pools and a "children's zone". Golf, horse riding, walking tours and scuba diving can be organized by staff.

Hotel Dom Pedro Marina
MAP H5 ▪ Rua Tivoli, Vilamoura ▪ (289) 300 780 ▪ www.dompedro. com ▪ €€
With its own exclusive beach area next to Vilamoura marina, this is a popular choice. Childcare is available, and facilities for adults include pools and a restaurant specializing in fine Italian cuisine.

Pestana Alvor Park
MAP D5 ▪ Quinta do Ribeiro, Alvor ▪ (282) 000 500 ▪ www.pestana. com ▪ €€
An attractive aparthotel and villa complex. Its facilities include indoor and outdoor pools, a sauna, gym and a games room. A children's fun centre is complemented by nearby golf, tennis and watersports facilities.

Vila Galé Albacora
MAP M4 ▪ Quatro Águas, Tavira ▪ (281) 380 800 ▪ www.vilagale. com ▪ €€
A children's club and entertainment, plus two swimming pools, a diving centre and the wonderful beaches at Ilha de Tavira make this hotel perfect for families.

The Lake Spa Resort
MAP H5 ▪ Praia da Falésia, Vilamoura ▪ (289) 320 700 ▪ www. thelakeresort.com ▪ €€€
One of the pools here is designed as a shallow lake with a sandy beach. Spacious apartments are available, and there is a spa and three restaurants. Baby-sitting services are available, and youngsters can enjoy the activities at the Koala Club.

Martinhal Beach Resort & Hotel

MAP B6 ▪ Quinta do Martinhal, near Sagres ▪ (282) 240 200 ▪ www.martinhal.com ▪ €€€

Ideal for families with children of all ages, this resort offers spacious and stylishly designed accommodation. The restaurants and spa are also family-friendly. The fashionable hotel section is more suited to couples.

Boutique Places to Stay

Aldeia da Pedralva

MAP B4 ▪ Pedralva, north of Vila do Bispo ▪ (282) 639 342 ▪ No air conditioning ▪ www.aldeiadapedralva.com ▪ €€

An entire country village has been carefully restored to offer self-catering stays in wonderfully authentic whitewashed cottages overlooking pretty countryside. Members of staff are all friendly and helpful, and there is also a handy shop and an on-site bar and restaurant.

Fazenda Nova Country House

MAP M4 ▪ Estiramentens, Santo Estevão ▪ (281) 961 913 ▪ www.fazenda nova.eu ▪ €€

Set in a pretty valley, this British-run Portuguese country house has self-contained apartments and ten large suites – nine with a private garden or terrace. Traditional architecture is combined with fresh and contemporary interior design, and the grounds are delightful.

Forte de São João da Barra

MAP N4 ▪ Barroca, Cabanas ▪ (960) 375 419 ▪ No air conditioning ▪ www.fortesaojoaoda barra.com ▪ €€

This beautifully refurbished and secluded 17th-century fort overlooks the crystal-blue lagoons of the Ria Formosa. The grounds incorporate a plunge pool. Call for directions.

Pousada de Tavira – Convento da Graça

MAP M4 ▪ Rua D. Paio Peres Correia, Tavira ▪ (281) 329 040 ▪ www.pousadas.pt ▪ €€

Housed in a stunningly refurbished, 16th-century convent replete with cloisters, the pousada's modern rooms overlook a pool and the old town walls. Guest amenities include the Magic Wellness centre and a notable Portuguese restaurant.

Quinta das Achadas

MAP D4 ▪ Estrada da Barragem, Odiáxere ▪ (282) 798 425 ▪ No air conditioning ▪ www.algarveholiday.net ▪ €€

This refurbished family-run farmhouse is set in wonderful gardens on a tranquil, 3-hectare site. There is a swimming pool, an outdoor Jacuzzi and a children's play area. A communal dinner is prepared twice a week.

Quinta do Caracol

MAP M4 ▪ Rua de São Pedro, Tavira ▪ (281) 322 475 ▪ www.quintado caracol.com ▪ €€

A 17th-century farm that has been converted into a series of beautiful apartments, each named after flowers. Birdsong

from the garden aviary drifts through the outdoor dining areas.

Vila Valverde Design & Country House

MAP C5 ▪ Estrada da Praia da Luz, Valverde ▪ (282) 790 790 ▪ No disabled access ▪ www.vilavalverde.com ▪ €€

A boutique hotel with 15 individually designed rooms. Amenities include heated indoor and outdoor pools, plus a fitness centre.

Quinta Bonita

MAP D5 ▪ Matos Morenos, Quatro Estradas, near Lagos ▪ (282) 762 135 ▪ www.boutiquehotel algarve.com ▪ €€€

Embedded in landscaped grounds, this peaceful retreat combines traditional character with luxurious boutique flourishes. There is an enticing outside pool.

Hotels with Golf Courses

Amendoeira Golf Resort

MAP F4 ▪ Morgado da Lameira ▪ (282) 320 820 ▪ www.amendoeira resort.com ▪ €€

Fully equipped, self-catering apartments and villas with pools. The clubhouse features a restaurant and a golf academy, and overlooks the Faldo and O'Connor Jnr layouts. A free shuttle bus to the beach operates in July and August.

Morgado Golf & Country Club

MAP E4 ▪ Morgado do Reguengo ▪ (282) 241 540 ▪ www.nauhotels.com ▪ €€

All 98 rooms at this stylish hotel overlook

the Morgado Golf Course. Guests have the use of four swimming pools, and a kid's club functions between July and September. Views from the restaurant and bars take in the region's rustic hinterland.

Penina Hotel & Golf Resort

MAP E4 ▪ Penina, near Portimão ▪ (282) 420 200 ▪ www.penina.com ▪ €€
Guests at this luxury resort can enjoy the use of the 18-hole, Sir Henry Cotton layout, which has hosted the Portuguese Open several times. There are also two 9-hole courses (see p60).

Pestana Vila Sol Golf & Resort

MAP J5 ▪ Morgadinhos, near Vilamoura ▪ (289) 320 320 ▪ www.pestana.com ▪ €€
A renowned 18-hole Championship golf course designed by architect Donald Steel meanders around this five-star resort via several exciting water features.

Dona Filipa & San Lorenzo Golf Resort

MAP J5 ▪ Vale do Lobo, Almancil ▪ (289) 357 200 ▪ www.donafilipahotel.com ▪ €€€
This resort offers five-star accommodation, and priority of play at the par 72 scenic masterpiece is offered to hotel guests.

Monte Rei Golf & Country Club

MAP N4 ▪ Sítio do Pocinho, Sesmarias ▪ (281) 950 950 ▪ www.monte-rei.com ▪ €€€
Short-term villa rentals at this serene country

club make it ideal for small groups or families. Exclusive leisure amenities include swimming pools, tennis courts, a spa and fine dining. There is also the peerless Jack Nicklaus-designed championship golf course (see p61).

Pine Cliffs Hotel

MAP G5 ▪ Praia da Falésia, Albufeira ▪ (289) 500 100 ▪ www.pinecliffs.com ▪ €€€
The hotel has a spectacular clifftop course (see p60). The course and luxury hotel form the hub of the exclusive Pine Cliffs resort.

Mid-Range Hotels

Eurotel Altura

MAP P4 ▪ Avenida 24 de Junho, Altura ▪ (281) 956 450 ▪ www.eurotel-altura.com ▪ €€
With a perfect location by the ocean, this smart, family-friendly resort offers rooms that face the ocean. Facilities include a wellness center, spa, tennis court and a children's club. The Quinta da Ria golf course is nearby.

Hotel Eva

MAP K6 ▪ Avenida da República, 1, Faro ▪ (289) 001 000 ▪ www.ap-hotelsresorts.com ▪ €€
Hotel Eva is very comfortable and conveniently situated right on Faro's marina. The panorama from the rooftop swimming pool is outstanding and takes in the Ria Formosa. The city's historic old quarter is a 5-minute walk away.

Hotel Jupiter

MAP E5 ▪ Avenida Tomás Cabreira 92, Praia da Rocha ▪ (282) 470 470 ▪ www.jupiteralgarvehotel.com ▪ €€
Superbly appointed throughout, Hotel Jupiter's beachfront accommodation includes "Deluxe" rooms, which enjoy majestic ocean views. An excellent spa offers a hydrotherapy circuit, among other treatments. There is a fitness room and indoor and outdoor pools (covered over in winter). The restaurant serves delicious regional cuisine.

Hotel Termal, Villa Termal das Caldas de Monchique Spa Resort

MAP E3 ▪ Caldas de Monchique ▪ (282) 910 910 ▪ www.monchiquetermas.com ▪ €€
One of five hotel options within the Villa Termal das Caldas de Monchique Spa Resort, Hotel Termal's 36 "Essencial" rooms are classically styled and afford pleasing views over the gardens and surrounding woodland.

Memmo Baleeira

MAP B6 ▪ Sítio da Baleeira, Sagres ▪ (282) 624 212 ▪ www.memmohotels.com ▪ €€
Memmo's stylish rooms enjoy picturesque garden and harbour views. Facilities include an excellent restaurant, spa, gym and a pool. There is also a surf centre where outdoor activities can be booked. Reservations are recommended for August.

For a key to hotel price categories see p124

Porto Bay Falésia

MAP H5 ■ Quinta do Milharo, near Olhas de Agua ■ (289) 007 700 ■ www.portobay.com ■ €€

Overlooking the picturesque Praia da Falésia *(see p85)*, this family-friendly resort's prime location is complemented by a glorious outdoor pool surrounded by verdant gardens. The dining experience includes the Mediterranean-themed Il Basílico Restaurant.

Pousada Palácio de Estói

MAP K5 ■ Palácio de Estói, Estói ■ (289) 990 150 ■ www.pousadas.pt ■ €€

The ancestral home of the Viscount of Estói has been carefully renovated. A contemporary wing was attached to create a luxurious pousada with ceiling murals, a spa, a swimming pool and French gardens.

Tivoli Carvoeiro

MAP E5 ■ Vale do Covo, Carvoeiro ■ (282) 351 100 ■ www.tivolihotels.com ■ €€

Commanding views over precipitous cliffs, this hotel is within walking distance of Carvoeiro town centre. The interior is Moorish in influence, and some rooms have spectacular ocean vistas. The health club has a Jacuzzi, sauna and Turkish bath, and there is a diving school nearby.

Tivoli Lagos

MAP D5 ■ Rua António Crisógono dos Santos, Lagos ■ (282) 790 079 ■ www.tivolihotels.com ■ €€

Near the old town, this smart hotel comprises a series of buildings set around a swimming pool. Guests also have the use of an exclusive beach club on the seafront.

Vila Monte

MAP L5 ■ Sítio dos Caliços, Moncarapacho ■ (289) 790 790 ■ www.vilamonte.com ■ €€

A rustic-chic design defines this upmarket boutique property, located 15 minutes inland from the beach. Housed in different buildings, the rooms and suites are stylishly furnished. Guest amenities extend to the homely À Terra restaurant *(see p95)*. Other activities include yoga, hiking, horseback riding, golf lessons and dolphin-watching.

Value for Money

Albergaria Vila Lido

MAP E5 ■ Avenida Tomás Cabreira, Praia da Rocha ■ (282) 424 127 ■ Closed mid-Oct–Mar ■ www.vilalido.pt ■ €

Overlooking the beach, this charming villa, with its distinctive blue window shutters, exudes grace and elegance. Rooms are light and airy and offer either sea or garden views. Breakfast is eaten on a beautiful veranda.

Alte Hotel

MAP H3 ■ Estrada de Santa Margarida, Alte ■ (289) 478 523 ■ www.altehotel.com ■ €

Alte is one of the prettiest villages in the Algarve, surrounded by the Serra do Caldeirão mountains. The views from the hotel are stunning, although its position at the summit of a hill means that having your own transport is useful. Leisure amenities include a swimming pool, tennis court and billiards.

Hotel Colina dos Mouros

MAP F4 ■ Pocinho Santo, Silves ■ (282) 340 470 ■ Closed Nov–Mar ■ www.colinahotels.com ■ €

There is a great view of Silves castle from this friendly hotel, just a few minutes' walk from the historic quarter. A sun terrace overlooks a circular pool and rows of orange groves.

Hotel Residencial Salema

MAP C5 ■ Rua 28 de Janeiro, Salema ■ (282) 695 328 ■ www.hotelsalema.com ■ €

The hotel building is the centrepiece of an old quay that retains the charm of colourful boats and rows of fishermen's huts. The rooms have views of the bay, and there are many bars, restaurants and cafés nearby.

Loulé Jardim

MAP J4 ■ Praça Manuel de Arriaga, 8100 Loulé ■ (289) 413 095 ■ www.loulejardimhotel.com ■ €

Refurbished to an early 20th-century design, the mustard-and-cream façade faces a quiet park in the centre of Loulé. The town's castle and Saturday market are both within easy reach, and the rooftop pool is a bonus.

Alcazar Hotel

MAP P4 ■ Rua de Ceuta 9, Monte Gordo ■ (281) 510 140 ■ www.hotelalcazaralgarve.com ■ €€

With clean and comfortable beachfront rooms, this

hotel is ideal for couples. It has won praise for its excellent customer service and hearty breakfasts. There is a bar and two outdoor pools. A perfect base from which to explore the eastern Algarve.

Casa da Moura

MAP D5 ▪ Rua Cardeal Neto 10, Lagos ▪ (967) 177 590 ▪ www.casa damoura.com ▪ €€
The interior design of this 100-year-old manor house reflects a colourful Moorish style. A tiled patio garden surrounds a small swimming pool. The breakfast terrace affords fine views over the old town walls.

Vila São Vicente

MAP G5 ▪ Largo Jacinto D'Ayet, Albufeira ▪ (289) 583 700 ▪ www.hotelsao vicentealbufeira.com ▪ €€
This traditionally-styled boutique property has rooms with terraces or balconies, and some with glorious ocean views. A modest swimming pool is sunk into the outside patio. The beach, old town and marina (see p37) are a 10-minute walk away.

Budget Hotels

Casa Beny

MAP J4 ▪ Rua São Domingos 13, Loulé ▪ (289) 417 702 ▪ No credit cards ▪ Breakfast not included ▪ €
A smart property, located in the centre of Loulé. The sleek, well-appointed rooms all have a TV and fridge, and guests also have access to a very handy rooftop terrace, where superb views of the castle can be enjoyed.

Pensão Bicuar Residencial

MAP L5 ▪ Rua Vasco da Gama 5, Olhão ▪ (289) 714 816 ▪ No credit cards ▪ No air conditioning ▪ www.pensionbicuar. com ▪ €
Centrally located, this self-catering budget option offers different room categories, all with a private shower. There is a fully equipped guest kitchen and complimentary Wi-Fi.

Pensão Luar

MAP C1 ▪ Rua da Várzea 28, Odeceixe ▪ (282) 947 194 ▪ No credit cards ▪ No air conditioning ▪ €
Some of the rooms here overlook the sweeping River Seixe valley, and this friendly pensão is ideal for the beach at Odeceixe. While secluded, this area is popular in summer, so booking is advisable.

Residência Matos Pereira

MAP P4 ▪ Rua Dr Sousa Martins 57, Vila Real de Santo António ▪ (281) 543 325 ▪ No credit cards ▪ Air conditioning in some rooms ▪ www. residenciamatospereira. com ▪ €
Set in a pedestrianized street, the Residência looks like a typical town house, and is matched by an atmosphere that is both domestic and jovial.

Residencial Lagôas

MAP M4 ▪ Rua Almirante Cândido dos Reis 24, Tavira ▪ (281) 328 243 ▪ No credit cards ▪ No air conditioning ▪ €
Polished black and white azulejos adorn the façade of this pensão. Its proximity to the historic centre of Tavira makes it

very popular in summer, so telephone ahead to check room availability.

Residencial Miradouro da Serra

MAP E3 ▪ Rua Combatentes do Ultramar, Monchique ▪ (282) 912 163 ▪ No air conditioning ▪ www.miradourodaserra. com ▪ €
The hotel name means "mountain viewpoint" and the panorama from this hilltop hideaway does not disappoint. The rooms are excellent value and the place makes a great base for hill walking or for simply pottering about in the pleasant market town of Monchique. All rooms have balcony views.

Residencial Pensão Limas

MAP G5 ▪ Rua da Liberdade, 25–7, Albufeira ▪ (289) 514 025 ▪ No credit cards ▪ Breakfast not included ▪ www.limasresidencial. com ▪ €
Wedged between bars and restaurants in a narrow, pedestrianized street, Limas's bright yellow awnings grace a whitewashed façade. The staircase inside is steep and narrow, and leads to modest bedrooms.

Residencial Ponte Romana

MAP F4 ▪ Ponte Romana, Silves ▪ (282) 443 275 ▪ No credit cards ▪ Break-fast not included ▪ €
Standing by the Roman bridge on the south side of the River Arade, this location is hard to beat. The riverside rooms face the castle. The restaurant serves generous portions of delicious country food.

Sol Algarve
MAP K6 ■ Rua Infante
D. Henrique 52, Faro
■ (289) 895 700 ■ www.
hotelsolalgarve.com ■ €
All 38 rooms at this
cheery establishment are
en suite, and most have a
balcony. When it is sunny,
breakfast can be eaten
in an attractive inner
courtyard. Free Wi-Fi.

Casa Azul
MAP B6 ■ Rua D.
Sebastião, Sagres
■ (282) 624 856 ■ €€
Stylish, bright and
colourful, this superior
guesthouse has captured
the imagination of surfers
and city slickers alike. Its
central position makes it
ideal for Sagres' buzzing
nightlife. Advance booking
is recommended.

Character Hostels and B&Bs

Amazigh Design Hostel
MAP C3 ■ Rua da Ladeira
5, Aljezur ■ (282) 997 502
■ Breakfast not included
■ www.amazighostel.com
■ €
A stylish budget option
configured with multi-bed
dorms and private double
rooms, all heated and
with private bathrooms.
A fully equipped kitchen
provides self-catering
facilities. Public areas
feature free Wi-Fi and
plasma TVs.

City Stork Hostel
MAP E4 ■ Rua Direita
70, Portimão ■ (962)
327 792 ■ www.city
storkhostel.com
■ €
Family-run and named
after the white storks
nesting on a nearby
chimneystack, the hostel
enjoys a great location
near the riverfront. The
double rooms and dorms
have their own bathroom
facilities, but guests share
a kitchen. Breakfast is
included in the price.

Loulé Coreto Hostel
MAP J4 ■ Avenida José
da Costa Mealha 68,
Loulé ■ (966) 660 943
■ www.loulecoreto
hostel.com ■ €
Male and female dorms
and private rooms are
available in a quiet and
tastefully decorated
environment, serviced
to hotel standards.
Bathroom and kitchen
facilities are shared, and
a buffet breakfast is
served daily. Free Wi-Fi.

Quinta da Tapada do Gramacho
MAP E4 ■ Sítio Tapada
do Gramacho, Silves
■ (919) 667 048 ■ Closed
Nov–Mar ■ www.tapada
dogramacho.com ■ €
A traditional farmhouse
has been renovated into
this chic, rustic hideaway.
Comprising of uniquely
designed, en suite, self-
catering apartments and
B&B suites, the *quinta's*
amenities extend to a
communal kitchen and
lounge, and an exterior
swimming pool.

Casa Beleza do Sul
MAP M4 ■ Rua Doutor
Parreira 43, Tavira ■ (960)
060 906 ■ www.casa
belezadosul.com ■ €€
Three suites and one
studio, all with a
kitchenette, occupy this
lovingly restored,
19th-century town house.
Individually styled and
utterly beguiling, each
room has access to a
patio terrace. There is
also a larger roof terrace
with wonderful views.
Breakfast is optional.

Casa Modesta
MAP L5 ■ Quatrim do
Sul, near Olhão ■ (289)
701 096/(964) 738 824
■ www.casamodesta.pt
■ €€
A striking example
of a modern makeover,
this lovely guesthouse
set in countryside over-
looking the Ria Formosa
Estuary has nine suites,
some with a private ter-
race and a kitchenette.
The garden features
a pool and a solarium.
Dinner is prepared
on request.

Casa Rosada
MAP P3 ■ Rua Dr Silvestre
Falcão 6-10, Castro Marim
■ (281) 544 215 ■ No
credit cards ■ www.casa
rosada-algarve.com ■ €€
A tangible air of tranquillity
pervades Casa Rosada's
interior, and with just three
individually furnished bedrooms provided, its appeal
is delightfully understated.
It is ideal for couples, who
are welcomed as family.
Breakfast is healthy and
wholesome and served
in the garden.

Quinta do Mel
MAP G5 ■ Olhos D'Água,
Albufeira ■ (289) 543 674
■ www.quintadomel.com
■ €€
This secluded rural
retreat offers ten attractive rooms, each with
a private bathroom.
Comforts include TV and
free internet. A pool is
set in the landscaped
grounds, artisan farm
produce is sold in the
teashop and a restau-
rant complements
the breakfast offer.

Vilafoîa
MAP E3 ▪ Corte Pereiro, Monchique ▪ (282) 910 110 ▪ www.vilafoia.com ▪ €€

A smart, modern B&B option set deep in woodland and ideal for exploring the Monchique hills. Rooms and studios are well appointed and enjoy splendid countryside views. The well-manicured gardens feature a salt-water swimming pool.

Campsites

Albufeira Camping
MAP G5 ▪ Estrada de Ferreiras, Albufeira ▪ (289) 587 629 ▪ www.campingalbufeira.net ▪ €

A sprawling camping and caravan site about 2 km (1 mile) from town, with three pools, an adventure playground, an à la carte restaurant, a supermarket and a nightclub.

Camping Olhão
MAP L5 ▪ Pinheiros de Marim, Apartado 300, Olhão ▪ (289) 700 300 ▪ www.sbfi.pt ▪ €

This excellent site near the Parque Natural da Ria Formosa has first-class amenities and lively recreation facilities that include a swimming pool and a tennis court. There is also a mini-market, a restaurant and a bar.

Parque de Campismo de Armação de Pêra
MAP F5 ▪ Parque de Campismo de Armação de Pêra ▪ (282) 312 260 ▪ www.camping-armacao-pera.com ▪ €

The nearest campsite to Armação de Pêra, this is great for budget travellers who crave the sights and nightlife of a lively resort. Modern facilities abound and it is also possible to rent bungalows.

Parque de Campismo de Monte Gordo
MAP P4 ▪ Monte Gordo ▪ (281) 510 970 ▪ www.eurocampings.co.uk ▪ €

The conifer woodland near this campsite is home to the largest population of Mediterranean chameleon in Portugal. The walks here are superb, and Monte Gordo itself is a thriving town with a beach that has perfect conditions for sunbathing and swimming.

Parque de Campismo Muncipal da Ilha de Tavira
MAP M5 ▪ Ilha de Tavira ▪ (281) 320 580 ▪ Closed Oct–May ▪ No credit cards ▪ €

This island is car- and caravan-free; only tents are allowed. There are supermarket and restaurant facilities, and tent hire is possible too. The island is reached via ferry at Quatro Águas. The site is hugely popular in summer, so it is definitely best to book ahead.

Parque de Campismo Sagres
MAP B6 ▪ Cerro das Moitas, Sagres ▪ (282) 624 371 ▪ www.orbitur.pt ▪ €

It is not uncommon to see surfboards outside the tents and cabins here, as the campsite is within easy reach of some very fine surfing beaches. The amenities are excellent, and Sagres town is just less than 2 km (1 mile) away.

Parque de Campismo São Miguel
MAP C1 ▪ São Miguel, near Odeceixe ▪ (282) 947 145 ▪ www.campingsaomiguel.com ▪ €

Secluded under a canopy of pine, this is one of the most modern and well-equipped camping sites in southern Portugal. Facilities include tennis courts, a swimming pool, a supermarket and a restaurant, and the surrounding countryside is a national park. Sleek and modern caravans and bungalows can also be rented.

Parque de Campismo Serrão
MAP C3 ▪ Herdade do Serrão, Aljezur ▪ (282) 990 220 ▪ www.campingserrao.com ▪ €

This friendly camp and caravan site is conveniently located near some of the western Algarve's very best beaches. The facilities include a large swimming pool and a series of bungalows to rent, two of which offer wheelchair access.

Salema Eco Camp
MAP C5 ▪ Parque de Campismo, Quinta dos Carriços, Praia da Salema, Budens ▪ (282) 695 201 ▪ www.salemaecocamp.com ▪ €

Set in a pretty valley, this campsite offers all the necessary facilities – toilets, hot showers, laundry rooms, shops and a restaurant. There are modern studios and apartments for rent as well as the tent pitches.

For a key to hotel price categories see p124

General Index

Page numbers in **bold** refer to main entries

Acknowledgments

Author
Paul Bernhardt is a freelance travel writer, blogger and photographer who lives in Portugal.

Publishing Director Georgina Dee

Publisher Vivien Antwi

Design Director Phil Ormerod

Editorial Sophie Adam, Michelle Crane, Dipika Dasgupta, Rebecca Flynn, Rachel Fox, Ruth Reisenberger, Sally Schafer

Cover Design Bess Daly, Maxine Pedliham

Design Rahul Kumar, Marisa Renzullo

Picture Research Susie Peachey, Ellen Root, Lucy Sienkowska, Oran Tarjan

Cartography Zafar-ul-Islam Khan, Suresh Kumar, James Macdonald, Casper Morris

DTP Jason Little

Production Nancy-Jane Maun

Factchecker Mark Harding

Proofreader Laura Walker

Indexer Hilary Bird

First edition created by Blue Island Publishing, London

Revisions Sumita Khatwani, Shikha Kulkarni, Bandana Paul, Kanika Praharaj, Anuroop Sanwalia, Ankita Sharma, Tanveer Zaidi

Commissioned Photography Paul Bernhardt, Will Heap, William Reavell, Rough Guides/ Eddie Gerald, /Matthew Hancock, Linda Whitwam

Picture Credits
The publisher would like to thank the following for their kind permission to reproduce their photographs:
Key: a-above; b-below/bottom; c-centre; f-far; l-left; r-right; t-top

123RF.com: lianem 110b.

4Corners: Michael Howard 45b, 62b; SIME/ Olimpio Fantuz 49cr, 58t.

À Terra, Vila Monte: Nick Bayntun 95cra.

Adega do Cantor: Birchphotography.com/Dan Birch 37tl, 54br.

Alamy Stock Photo: age fotostock/Salva Garrigues 31tr; Arco Images GmbH 44bc, / Therin-Weise 18-9; The Art Archive/Gianni Dagli Orti 42br; Greg Balfour Evans 7tl, 74b; Paul Bernhardt 14crb; Bildagentur-online 16-7; blickwinkel/McPHOTO/ZAG 48tr; Ian Bottle 50cra; Buiten-Beeld/Nico van Kappel 33tr; Andy Christiani 10cb; Carl DeAbreu 27cra; DIGITEYES 2tr, 40-1; edpics 10tr; eye35 34-5, 104tl; eye35 stock 45cla; eye35.

pix 3tr, 27tl, 114-5; Stephen French 10b; Gastromedia/Gastrofotos 70bl; GM Photo Images 16bl; André Vicente Gonçalves 88clb; hemis.fr/Philippe Blanchot 56tr, /René Mattes 1; The History Collection 43tl; Jam World Images 4cla; Christa Knijff 42cla; Hideo Kurihara 111br; Kuttig - RF - Travel 2tl, 8-9; LOOK Die Bildagentur der Fotografen GmbH 22clb; LusoWine 112t; Johnny Madsen 32br; Cro Magnon 4clb, 4b, 17crb, 28t, 38clb, 46br, 47tl, 92b, 108bl; Stephen Meese 11cb; MicaSelects 38-9; tony mills 32tl; Novarc Images/Miguel Caibarien 43br; pbucknall 60b; LOOK Die Bildagentur der Fotografen GmbH/ Roetting/ Pollex 19tl; Simon Reddy 71clb; Phil Rees 74cl; Robertharding/Neale Clark 35tc; Mauro Rodrigues 76tl, 77br; Rymar 23br; Kumar Sriskandan 18cl; Travel Pictures/ Pictures Colour Library 50bl; travelpixs 39clb; Duncan Usher 32c; Visions from Earth 64-5, 96-7; Washington Imaging 4t; Westend61 GmbH/Mel Stuart 31bl, /Michael Reusse 59l; Jan Wlodarczyk 4crb.

Algarve Classic Car Festival: 76cr.

Apolónia Supermercados: 87br.

Associação Turismo do Algarve: 20-1, 59b, 94b, 98tl.

Autodromo Internacional de Algarve: A. Fernandes 38br.

AWL Images: Sabine Lubenow 62tl.

Paul Bernhardt: 13tl, 17tc.

Boutique Hotel Vivenda Miranda: 72br.

Cacto: 105cl.

Câmara Municipal de Lagos: Carlos Afonso 28bl, Lagos Museu Municipal 29cl.

Casa Velha: 72tl.

Corbis: Lou Avers 15c; JAI/Mauricio Abreu 100b; Wolfgang Kaehler 29tr.

Dreamstime.com: Ahfotobox 103b; Ilia Aleksandrov 85tr; Altezza 6cla, 12clb; Amabrao 63crb; Anitasstudio 48b; Anyaivanova 83cl; Philip Bird 91bl; Olena Buyskykh 102cl; Valeria Cantone 57crb; Carlos Neto 93cl; Dmitry Chulov 90tl; Wessel Cirkel 60cla; Compuinfoto 111tl, 75br; Cw24044 4t; Devy 26cra, 99t; Rene Drouyer 81t; Peter Etchells 26clb; Fabiomsantos 30-1, Ferragudo in the Algarve Portugal 51t; Fosterss 77cl; Armando Frazão 16cl; G0r3cki 30cl; Rafał Gadomski 10cla, 34clb; Golasza 4cl, 15bl; Hectorsnchz 107b; Marianne De Jong 100tl; Jacek Kadaj 99cr; Lianem 109cl, 110cla; Madrugadaverde 3tl, 78-9; Mkos83 24-5; Aitor Muñoz Muñoz 35crb, 108t; Murdock2013 20cra; Elena Pavlova 67br; Pkazmierczak 26br, 44cla, 51clb, 52-3; Ppy2010ha 70cla; Presse750 12br; Radaway 38cla; Mauro Rodrigues 4cr, 61clb; Ruigouveia 82-3; Saiko3p 12-3c, 106cla, 107tr; Rui G. Santos 56b; Sebastian423 84cl; Richard Semik 109bl;

Sergioua 101cl; Hans Slegers 59t; Steirus 66crb; Ronalds Stikans 11bl; Vvoevale 14tl; Steve Woods 22-3; Rudmer Zwerver 61br.

Getty Images: AWL Images RM/Sabine Lubenow 58bl; Paul Bernhardt 55crb; Valter Jacinto 33br; Keystone-France/Gamma-Keystone 43clb; Sabine Lubenow 11cra, 91tr; VWB photos 7cra.

Grupo Liberto Mealha: 69tl.

Kadoc: 69b, 88tr.

Museu do Traje e São Brás de Alportel: 47br.

NoSoloÁgua Portimão: 68cl.

O Charneco: 89br.

Photoshot: Frank Fell 21c.

Pine Cliffs: 86t.

Porches Pottery: Brian P. Fortune 75c, 87c.

Pousadas de Portugal/Grupo Pestana: 113cl.

Quinta do Francês vineyard: 54cl.

Rex by Shutterstock: imageBROKER/Jürgen Wackenhut 61tl.

Robert Harding Picture Library: BAO 15tr, 92tl; Neale Clark 11tr, 36cla; Jurgen Wackenhut 11crb; Jan Wlodarczyk 36-7.

Slide and Splash: 67t.

Sueste: 73tl.

SuperStock: Stock Connection 85br.

Turismo de Portugal: Jose Manuel 12cla.

Vila Joya: 73crb.

Cover

Front and spine: **iStockphoto.com:** tonda.

Back: **AWL Images:** Sabine Lubenow tr; **Dreamstime.com:** Artem Evdokimov cla; Hlphoto tl; Rosshelen crb; **iStockphoto.com:** tonda bc.

Pull Out Map Cover

iStockphoto.com: tonda

All other images © Dorling Kindersley For further information see: www.dkimages.com

As a guide to abbreviations in visitor information blocks: **Adm** *= admission charge;* **D** *= dinner;* **L** *= lunch.*

Printed and bound in China

First edition 2003

Published in Great Britain by
Dorling Kindersley Limited
80 Strand, London WC2R 0RL

Published in the United States by
DK Publishing, 345 Hudson Street,
New York, New York 10014

Copyright © 2003, 2019 Dorling
Kindersley Limited

A Penguin Random House Company

18 19 20 21 10 9 8 7 6 5 4 3 2 1

Reprinted with revisions 2005, 2007, 2009, 2011, 2013, 2015, 2017, 2019

ISSN 1479-344X

ISBN 978-0-2413-5597-8

SPECIAL EDITIONS OF DK TRAVEL GUIDES

DK Travel Guides can be purchased in bulk quantities at discounted prices for use in promotions or as premiums. We also offer special editions and personalized jackets, corporate imprints, and excerpts from all our books, tailored specifically to meet your needs.

To find out more, please contact:

in the US
specialsales@dk.com
in the UK
travelguides@uk.dk.com
in Canada
specialmarkets@dk.com
in Australia
penguincorporatesales@ penguinrandomhouse.com.au

Phrase Book

In an Emergency

Help!	Socorro!	soo-koh-roo!
Stop!	Pára!	pahr'!
Call a doctor!	Chame um médico!	shahm' ooñ meh-dee-koo!
Call an ambulance!	Chame uma ambulância!	shahm' oo-muh añ-boo-lañ-see-uh!
Call the police!	Chame a polícia!	shahm' uh poo-lee-see-uh!
Call the fire brigade!	Chame os bombeiros!	shahm' oosh' bom-bay-roosh!
Where is the nearest telephone?	Há um telefone aqui perto?	ah ooñ te-le-fon' uh-kee pehr-too?
Where is the nearest hospital?	Onde é o hospital mais próximo?	ohsh-pee-tahl' mysh pro-see-moo?

Communication Essentials

Yes	Sim	seeñ
No	Não	nowñ
Please	Por favor/ Faz favor	poor fuh-vor fash fuh-vor
Thank you	Obrigado/da	o-bree-gah-doo/duh
Excuse me	Desculpe	dish-koolp'
Hello	Olá	oh-lah
Goodbye	Adeus	a-deh-oosh
Good morning	Bom-dia	boñ dee-uh
Good afternoon	Boa-tarde	boh-uh tard'
Good night	Boa-noite	boh-uh noyt'
Yesterday	Ontem	oñ-tayñ
Today	Hoje	ohj'
Tomorrow	Amanhã	ah-mañ yañ
Here	Aqui	uh-kee
There	Ali	uh-lee
What?	O quê?	oo keh?
Which?	Qual?	kwahl'?
When?	Quando?	kwañ-doo?
Why?	Porquê?	poor-keh?
Where?	Onde?	oñd'?

Useful Phrases

How are you?	Como está?	koh-moo shtah?
Very well, thank you.	Bem, obrigado/da.	bayñ, o-bree gah-doo/da.
Pleased to meet you.	Encantado/da.	eñ-kañ-tah-doo/ duh.
See you soon.	Até logo.	uh-teh loh-goo.
That's fine.	Está bem.	shtah bayñ.
Where is/are…?	Onde está/ estão…?	ond' shtah/ shtowñ…?
How far is it to…?	A que distância fica…?	uh kee dish-tañ-see-uh fee-kuh…?
Which way to…?	Como se vai para…?	koh-moo sh vy puh-ruh…?
Do you speak English?	Fala Inglês?	fah-luh eeñ-glehsh?
I don't understand.	Não compreendo.	nowñ kom-pree-eñ-doo.
I'm sorry.	Desculpe.	dish-koolp'
Could you speak more slowly, please?	Pode falar mais devagar, por favor?	pohd' fuh-lar mysh d'-va-gar, poor fah-vor?

Useful Words

big	grande	grañd'
small	pequeno	pe-keh-noo
hot	quente	keñt'
cold	frio	free-oo
good	bom	boñ
bad	mau	mah-oo
enough	bastante	bash-tañt'
well	bem	bayñ
open	aberto	a-behr-too
closed	fechado	fe-shah-doo
left	esquerda	shkehr-duh
right	direita	dee-ray-tuh
straight on	em frente	ayñ freñt'
near	perto	pehr-too
far	longe	loñj'
up	suba	soo-bah
down	desça	deh-shuh
early	cedo	seh-doo
late	tarde	tard'
entrance	entrada	eñ-trah-duh
exit	saída	sa-ee-duh
toilets	casa de banho	kah-zuh d' bañ-yoo
more	mais	mysh
less	menos	meh-noosh

Making a Telephone Call

I'd like to place an international call.	Queria fazer uma chamada internacional.	kree-uh fuh-zehr oo-muh sha-mah-duh in-ter-na-see-oo-nahl'.
a local call	uma chamada local	oo-muh sha-mah-duh loo-kahl'
Can I leave a message?	Posso deixar uma mensagem?	poh-soo day-shar oo-muh meñ-sah-jayñ?

Shopping

How much does this cost?	Quanto custa isto?	kwañ-too koosh-tuh eesh-too?
I would like…	Queria…	kree-uh…
I'm just looking.	Estou só a ver obrigado/a.	shtoh soh vehr o-bree-gah-doo/uh.
Do you take credit cards?	Aceita cartões de crédito?	uh-say-tuh kar-toinsh de kreh-dee-too?
What time do you open?	A que horas abre?	uh kee oh-rash ah-bre?
What time do you close?	A que horas fecha?	uh kee oh-rash fay-shuh?
this one	este	ehst'
that one	esse	ehss'
expensive	caro	kah-roo
cheap	barato	buh-rah-too
size (clothes/ shoes)	número	noom'-roo
white	branco	brañ-koo
black	preto	preh-too
red	vermelho	ver-melh-yoo
yellow	amarelo	uh-muh-reh-loo
green	verde	vehrd'
blue	azul	uh-zool'

Types of Shop

antique shop	loja de antiguidades	*loh-juh de añ-tee-gwee-dahd'sh*
bakery	padaria	*pah-duh-ree-uh*
bank	banco	*bañ-koo*
bookshop	livraria	*lee-vruh-ree-uh*
butcher	talho	*tah-lyoo*
cake shop	pastelaria	*pash-te-luh-ree-uh*
chemist	farmácia	*far-mah-see-uh*
fishmonger	peixaria	*pay-shuh-ree-uh*
hairdresser	cabeleireiro	*kab'-lay-ray-roo*
market	mercado	*mehr-kah-doo*
newsagent	kiosque	*kee-yohsk'*
post office	correios	*koo-ray-oosh*
shoe shop	sapataria	*suh-puh-tuh-ree-uh*
supermarket	supermercado	*soo-pehr-mer-kah-doo*
tobacconist	tabacaria	*tuh-buh-kuh-ree-uh*
travel agency	agência de viagens	*uh-jen-see-uh de vee-ah-jayñsh*

Sightseeing

cathedral	sé	*seh*
church	igreja	*ee-gray-juh*
garden	jardim	*jar-deeñ*
library	biblioteca	*bee-blee-oo-teh-kuh*
museum	museu	*moo-zeh-oo*
tourist information	posto de turismo	*posh-too d' too-reesh-moo*
closed for holidays	fechado para férias	*fe-sha-doo puh-ruh feh-ree-ash*
bus station	estação de autocarros	*shta-sowñ d' oh-too-kah-roosh*
railway station	estação de comboios	*shta-sowñ d' koñ-boy-oosh*
painted ceramic tile	azulejo	*uh-zoo-lay-joo*
Manueline (late Gothic architectural style)	Manuelino	*ma-noo-el-ee-oo*

Staying in a Hotel

Do you have a vacant room?	Tem um quarto livre?	*tayñ ooñ kwar-too leevr'?*
room with a bath	um quarto com casa de banho	*ooñ kwar-too koñ kah-zuh d' bañ-yoo*
shower	duche	*doosh*
single room	quarto individual	*kwar-too een-dee-vee-doo-ahl'*
double room	quarto de casal	*kwar-too d' kuh-zhal'*
twin room	quarto com duas camas	*kwar-too koñ doo-ash kah-mash*
porter	porteiro	*poor-tay-roo*
key	chave	*shahv'*
I have a reservation.	Tenho um quarto reservado.	*tayñ-yoo ooñ kwar-too re-ser-vah-doo.*

Eating Out

Have you got a table for …?	Tem uma mesa para …?	*tayñ oo-muh meh-zuh puh-ruh?*
I'd like to reserve a table.	Quero reservar una mesa.	*keh-roo re-zehr-var oo-muh meh-zuh.*
The bill, please.	A conta por favor/faz favor.	*uh kohn-tuh poor fuh-vor/fash fuh-vor.*
I am a vegetarian.	Sou vegetariano/a.	*Soh ve-je-tuh-ree-ah-noo/uh.*
Waiter!	Por favor!/Faz favor!	*poor fuh-vor!/fash fuh-vor!*
the menu	a lista	*uh leesh-tuh*
fixed-price menu	a ementa turística	*uh ee-mehñ-tuh too-reesh-tee-kuh*
wine list	a lista de vinhos	*uh leesh-tuh de veeñ-yoosh*
glass	um copo	*ooñ koh-poo*
bottle	uma garrafa	*oo-muh guh-rah-fuh*
half-bottle	meia-garrafa	*may-uh guh-rah-fuh*
knife	uma faca	*oo-mah fah-kuh*
fork	um garfo	*ooñ gar-foo*
spoon	uma colher	*oo-muh kool-yair*
plate	um prato	*ooñ prah-too*
breakfast	pequeno-almoço	*pe-keh-noo-ahl-moh-soo*
lunch	almoço	*ahl-moh-soo*
dinner	jantar	*jan-tar*
cover	couvert	*koo-vehr*
starter	entrada	*eñ-trah-duh*
main course	prato principal	*prah-too prin-see-pahl'*
dish of the day	prato do dia	*prah-too doo dee-uh*
set dish	combinado	*koñ-bee-nah-doo*
half-portion	meia-dose	*may-uh doh-se*
dessert	sobremesa	*soh-bre-meh-zuh*
rare	mal passado	*mahl' puh-sah-doo*
medium	médio	*meh-dee-oo*
well done	bem passado	*bayñ puh-sah-doo*

Menu Decoder

abacate	*uh-buh-kaht'*	avocado
açorda	*uh-sor-duh*	bread-based stew (often seafood)
açúcar	*uh-soo-kar*	sugar
água mineral	*ah-gwuh mee-ne-rahl'*	mineral water
alho	*ay-oo*	garlic
alperce	*ahl'-pehrce*	apricot
amêijoas	*uh-may-joo-ash*	clams
ananás	*uh-nuh-nahsh*	pineapple
arroz	*uh-rohsh*	rice
assado	*uh-sah-doo*	baked
atum	*uh-tooñ*	tuna
aves	*ah-vesh*	poultry
azeite	*uh-zayt'*	olive oil
azeitonas	*uh-zay-toh-nash*	olives
bacalhau	*buh-kuh-lyow*	dried, salted cod
banana	*buh-nah-nuh*	banana
batatas	*buh-tah-tash*	potatoes
batatas fritas	*buh-tah-tash free-tash*	French fries

batido	*buh-tee-doo*	milkshake
bica	*bee-kuh*	espresso
bife	*beef*	steak
bolacha	*boo-lah-shuh*	biscuit
bolo	*boh-loo*	cake
borrego	*boo-reh-goo*	lamb
caça	*kah-ssuh*	game
café	*kuh-feh*	coffee
camarões	*kuh-muh-roysh*	large prawns
caracóis	*kuh-ruh-koysh*	snails
carangueijo	*kuh-rañ-gay-yoo*	crabs
carne	*karn'*	meat
cataplana	*kuh-plah-nah*	sealed wok used to steam dishes
cebola	*se-boh-luh*	onion
cerveja	*sehr-vay-juh*	beer
chá	*shah*	tea
cherne	*shern'*	stone bass
chocolate	*shoh-koh-laht'*	chocolate
chocos	*shoh-koosh*	cuttlefish
chouriço	*shoh-ree-soo*	red, spicy sausage
churrasco	*shoo-rash-coo*	on the spit
cogumelos	*koo-goo-meh-loosh*	mushrooms
cozido	*koo-zee-doo*	boiled
enguias	*eñ-gee-ash*	eels
fiambre	*fee-añbr'*	ham
fígado	*fee-guh-doo*	liver
frango	*frañ-goo*	chicken
frito	*free-too*	fried
fruta	*froo-tah*	fruit
gambas	*gañ-bash*	prawns
gelado	*je-lah-doo*	ice cream
gelo	*jeh-loo*	ice
goraz	*goo-rash*	bream
grelhado	*grel-yah-doo*	grilled
iscas	*eesh-kash*	marinated liver
lagosta	*luh-gohsh-tuh*	lobster
laranja	*luh rañ-juh*	orange
leite	*layt'*	milk
limão	*lee-mowñ*	lemon
limonada	*lee-moo-nah-duh*	lemonade
linguado	*leeñ-gwah-doo*	sole
lulas	*loo-lash*	squid
maçã	*muh-sañ*	apple
manteiga	*mañ-tay-guh*	butter
marisco	*muh-reesh-koosh*	seafood
meia-de-leite	*may-uh-d' layt'*	white coffee
ostras	*osh-trash*	oysters
ovos	*oh-voosh*	eggs
pão	*powñ*	bread
pastel	*pash-tehl'*	cake
pato	*pah-too*	duck
peixe	*paysh'*	fish
peixe-espada	*paysh'-shpah-duh*	scabbard fish
pimenta	*pee-meñ-tuh*	pepper
polvo	*pohl'-voo*	octopus
porco	*por-coo*	pork
queijo	*kay-joo*	cheese
sal	*sahl'*	salt
salada	*suh-lah-duh*	salad
salsichas	*sahl-see-shash*	sausages
sandes	*sañ-desh*	sandwich
sopa	*soh-puh*	soup
sumo	*soo-moo*	juice
tamboril	*tañ-boo-ril'*	monkfish
tarte	*tart'*	pie/cake
tomate	*too-maht'*	tomato
torrada	*too-rah-duh*	toast
tosta	*tohsh-tuh*	toasted sandwich
vinagre	*vee-nah-gre*	vinegar
vinho branco	*veeñ-yoo brañ-koo*	white wine
vinho tinto	*veeñ-yoo teeñ-too*	red wine
vitela	*vee-teh-luh*	veal

Numbers

0	zero	*zeh-roo*
1	um	*ooñ*
2	dois	*doysh*
3	três	*tresh*
4	quatro	*kwa-troo*
5	cinco	*seeñ-koo*
6	seis	*saysh*
7	sete	*set'*
8	oito	*oy-too*
9	nove	*nov'*
10	dez	*desh*
11	onze	*oñz'*
12	doze	*doz'*
13	treze	*trez'*
14	catorze	*ka-torz'*
15	quinze	*keeñz'*
16	dezasseis	*de-zuh-saysh*
17	dezassete	*de-zuh-set'*
18	dezoito	*de-zoy-too*
19	dezanove	*de-zuh-nov'*
20	vinte	*veent'*
21	vinte e um	*veen-tee-ooñ*
30	trinta	*treeñ-tuh*
40	quarenta	*kwa-reñ-tuh*
50	cinquenta	*seen-kweñ-tuh*
60	sessenta	*se-señ-tuh*
70	setenta	*se-teñ-tuh*
80	oitenta	*oy-teñ-tuh*
90	noventa	*noo-veñ-tuh*
100	cem	*sayñ*
101	cento e um	*señ-too-ee-ooñ*
102	cento e dois	*señ-too-ee-doysh*
200	duzentos	*doo-zeñ-toosh*
300	trezentos	*tre-zeñ-toosh*
400	quatrocentos	*kwa-troo-señ-toosh*
500	quinhentos	*kee-nyeñ-toosh*
600	seiscentos	*saysh-señ-toosh*
700	setecentos	*set'-señ-toosh*
800	oitocentos	*oy-too-señ-toosh*
900	novecentos	*nov'-señ-toosh*
1,000	mil	*meel'*

Time

one minute	um minuto	*ooñ mee-noo-too*
one hour	uma hora	*oo-muh oh-ruh*
half an hour	meia-hora	*may-uh oh-ruh*
Monday	segunda-feira	*se-goon-duh-fay-ruh*
Tuesday	terça-feira	*ter-sa-fay-ruh*
Wednesday	quarta-feira	*kwar-ta-fay-ruh*
Thursday	quinta-feira	*keen-ta-fay-ruh*
Friday	sexta-feira	*say-shta-fay-ruh*
Saturday	sábado	*sah-ba-too*
Sunday	domingo	*doo-meen-goo*